Zen Running

Zen Running

by Leo Diporta

Everest House
Publishers
New York

Published simultaneously in Canada by Beaverbooks, Pickering, Ontario

ISBN: 0-89696-019-6

Library of Congress Catalog Card Number: 78-57416

INTRODUCTION

During the year when I passed from age forty-two to forty-three, the entire quality of my life was unexpectedly transformed.

I had originally set out to see if it was possible to translate what I knew of zen and dialectical philosophy into the action or "practice" of running. This was to be a personal experiment, conducted according to my experience as a professional social science scholar-researcher. Having been immersed for some time in scholarly works concerning zen and dialectics, and having also been doing conventional jogging and other sports in a haphazard fashion for many years, I began to perceive some connections between them. While trying to illustrate the concrete meaning of abstruse ideas to students, for example, I found myself more and more drawing upon experiences from skiing or tennis or sailing. And the students could reply in kind, using their own base of active experiences.

As this happened, I gradually formed the resolve to make a

deliberate effort to pursue the possible connection between what is ordinarily thought to be difficult, if not downright puzzling, philosophy and metaphysics on the one hand, and the most commonplace, if not dull-witted of human actions on the other. There is, after all, apparently nothing more monotonous or dull than just running, unless it is the meditation that zen masters call "just sitting."

The method was simple. I committed myself to try a year of serious running, through all the seasons and in various environments, focusing my concentration during each run upon whatever zen or dialectical principles would emerge. Moreover, as abstractions emerged, I would attempt to translate them into the actions of running; that is, the quality of the ideas would inform or dictate the quality of the running. Then, following each run, I very firmly resolved that despite any distraction, fatigue, or momentary apathy, I would note down what had happened, including a description of thoughts and feelings. And these notes, produced in this fashion, are given in the following pages.

The transformation process is apparent as one reads the notes. Indeed, the very style and format of the notes reflects the transformation, for they begin with a very global, almost arrogant series of observations, and they gradually shift to a much deeper level. As the running progressed and the winter weather made it much more difficult, the small things involved became more and more important. In fact, the running then began to instruct me as a zen master might instruct an apprentice, or as a dialectical philosopher might be instructed by close scrutiny of everyday practice.

After completing the notes, they lay untouched for a few months. On reading them again, having them read by two close friends, and pondering on the changes in my life that had accrued since the notes were finished—changes, I might say, that validate all the intimations of transformation perceived earlier on—I went over them, editing here and there for the sake of clarity, but making no basic changes. This material now appears as *Book I: The Running*. It is quite complete in itself, and says just about everything there is to say about the inner adventure or voyage of personal discovery that the running turned out to be.

Several months later, however, a different kind of inner adventure began, and this is recorded in Book II, called *The Sitting*.

It is simply a description of what happened to me during a year or so of zen meditation practice. It ties in very closely with the running experience, but goes much deeper. Indeed, it reveals that the running and sitting formed a perfect dialectical unity for me, opposite from one another, yet so intimately intertwined as to yield a single core meaning. As the Buddhist masters have said, "Not two; and not one, either."

The power of these two activities to profoundly change every significant aspect of my sense of being in the world is what this book is about. It is not entertainment. There are no funny stories, no interesting dramas, no long philosophical monologues; nothing about sex, violence, money, love, hate, or conventional notions of power. It is only a plain and mostly austere record of physical and mental experience with all ordinary interpersonal life detail deliberately stripped away, because it could happen to anyone, man or woman, plumber or professor. Jesus was a carpenter, Buddha was a prince. So I present this record as a specimen, a test-tube human experiment without any special personal identity attached to it. It is just the straight stuff: a hard, translucent, bottom-of-the-barrel precipitate containing what is left to life after all the waste has been boiled away.

"Many people are afraid to empty their minds lest they may plunge into the void. They do not know that their own Mind IS the void. The ignorant eschew phenomena but not thought; the wise eschew thought but not phenomena."

The Zen Teaching of Huang Po

"If you want to gain knowledge you must participate in the practice of changing reality."

Mao Tse-tung, *On Practice*

"The existence of the experimental method makes us think we have the means of solving the problems troubling us, even though problem and method pass one another by."

Ludwig Wittgenstein, *Philosophical Investigations*

BOOK ONE
THE RUNNING

1 BEGINNING THOUGHTS, JULY AND AUGUST

One sees the *Ground Pounders:* those who seek power by destruction and self-hate; the pain freaks, lost in the egotism of their guilt, trapped in a dialectic of thanatos, they seek to pound the earth into submission as they similarly pound upon their own body. They pervert the act of running into a form of capitalist enterprise, and exploit their bodies as the employers exploit labor, with no care for the future, no concern for the growing alienation between mind and body, and all to produce the profit of some seconds removed from their mile time. They destroy themselves soon enough.

THE RUNNING STEP.   Each running step is to be a matter of perfection. The impeccable step foretells the impeccable lap, and finally the impeccable run, that must end in harmony with its beginning. The dialectical running step draws energy from the earth as well as the body. Each step is a springing from the earth that contains within it the return to earth in the next step. Dialectical synthesis is in the floating between. One cannot float without a proper, perfect step, one cannot make perfect steps without a proper floating.

"LOSING THE SELF"; "NOT-DOING"; "SEE-ING"; "EXPERIENCING IT." All require rough ground, variations that destroy previous self-indulgences accumulated on conquered ground. Used or conquered ground loses its force to generate concentration. It is exhausted of vitality as it is subjected, bound, and made into a routine object by over-frequent use. The same track used day after day is made into an old whore with no power to excite, and the runner becomes no more than an old whore's familiar client.

RITUAL.   Ritual should begin on waking. Right breathing is the first act of correct ritual. The impeccable step is already implicit in the right breathing which focuses one's purpose to run. The morning time; awakening of the earth with the mind and body; the earth offers itself in its maximum richness during the morning hours. Noon running; the variation for contact with the sun is very good but better reserved for a master. It is very potent at noon because the runner must transduce and mediate the vitality of the earth and the heat of the sun. Here one runs with the dangers of heat exhaustion. Night running . . . greatest of dangers and so much so as to be an egotism. The earth is now enemy as well as energizer. It traps the feet. The mind is most easily deceived at night and thus is better given to rest or at most to a slower, meditative running.

A LIFE IS A RUN.   Unto death. The slowly achieved consciousness of self and even later the not-self as transducer, is the high point and then it becomes a slowing down; shorter and shorter floating times. The possibility in the end is, however, always there to be pursued: floating without running. Floating in being.

THE TAXONOMY OF RUNS. The head trip; the sensory stimulator; the nimble harmonizer or self-loser. Music and rhythm are in the breathing. Thinking; projecting the body through the given act. The impeccable step is projected from its vision in the mind. Controlling the feet with the fingers . . . spring-float with a flick of the fingers.

RUNNING WITH THE SHADOW. Which is more real, the I that sees the shadow or the shadow that sees the I? ˙

"It" is everywhere; therefore, it may be looked for anywhere. If you look everywhere . . . anywhere . . . and do not find it, what then? Perhaps "it" is a lie, or the master lies, or you look but cannot find because you cannot see.

The dialectical relationship between the self and the shadow: the running shadow tells how the self is running. By watching the shadow one sees how one is going and what one is doing, and may change and learn ways toward more perfect running through the dialogue of matching and fitting and comparing the inside sense of self as runner with the shadow reflection of one's running. The shadow may gradually impose itself as follows. By close watching of changes in the shadow one maintains close watch over self and makes changes in self.

The zen master looks on the surface to be just another peasant; Don Juan goes outwardly as a nondescript . . . in both, perfection is concealed.

BREATHING. The metaphor of the fish out of water in relation to the runner out of breath. Out of breath one is reduced to being as an object, a victim of the dialogue between self and earth . . . one who has gone to running as to war and been crushed.

To breathe with control and dignity throughout, even at the end, is to make an advance toward mastery.

Chest breathing (nose) vs. belly breathing (mouth). Dialectic: in one way, out the other. Rhythm: breathing in harmony with stepping. The cadence of stepping and breathing may become as one.

SELF-ABANDON.   Running the stadium bleachers and stairs. Running the seats (dialectic!) up, down and sideways. This is running with danger and serves the role of zen contests or ceremonial tests to determine the degree of progress made by students.

If the mind as entrepreneur or general has succeeded in fully exploiting the body, one may see the ultimate alienation, yet it can be a value for it may lead the apprentice toward understanding of the unity needed between mind and body.

Making up rhythms . . . cadences . . . beats . . . songs . . . this seems to be a spontaneous process as one attempts to run in a unitary, harmonious way.

POWER BURSTS.   The arms may act virtually of their own accord as pistons propelling one up hills or over impediments. The arms will fly the runner like wings; the faster the arms work, the stronger the foot rise and the easier the float. Hill-climbing is foot-arm harmony.

Dialectical running means that the running is dialogical in nature. There is a general dialogue and interpenetration between the mind and the body that encloses the dialogues between legs and arms, ears and eyes, ear and foot. The dynamic aspect of the interpenetration that "carries" the dialogue is rhythm; the beat or syncopation of breathing, foot steps, arm swings, finger moves, wrist flipping, heart-lung action and all of the various elements in motion.

"STOPPING THE WORLD"   is achieved in dialectical running somewhat in proportion to speed. That is, the faster the general rhythm, the more the world is stopped. One moves out into an area of being that becomes a kind of vacuum of consciousness. It is a certain kind of psychophysical space totally dominated by the beat of the run and overlaid only with as much of the pure sensory input as one may absorb at his discretion. The visual feasts of light, shadow, sky, trees, grass, are like spices on food: one takes them to taste reflexively and depending upon non-conscious forms of impulse. In this case, stopping the world means that time is lost partially in the rhythm and partially in the sense intakes: one's conventional time sense is also partially swamped by the total focus on rhythm and by the immersion in sensations of earth and sky.

BUILDING RESOLVE IS LIKE BUILDING A FIRE.

It is necessary to begin by finding the small, fragile twigs of intention and purpose, and then as they are laid down to nurture the emerging flame of action to run. Then the larger stuff of intention such as preliminary actions toward the run, can be fed into the glowing center.

Building intention is focusing energy. To awake in the morning with the heaviness of death throughout the body is to feel the absence of any focused energy. With initial thought of the run comes a very tentative, preliminary focus. The breathing is the first substantial act. The first deep chest breath opens the body in a very small way to the intention for action. Then comes initial movement. Concentration is extremely difficult in these early phases, but follows best if the mind has resolved on a course of action prior to the onset of sleep.

FOCUS OF ENERGY ON WAKING.

Bend a finger, then a fist; breathe tight and relax . . . The eyes are *not* the first part of the body to awaken, they are the last. The eyes resist hardest and can best be approached by building energy levels in other parts.

The move or change from sleep to waking is a key juncture point for the runner. In this experience one is moving between two states of being, and so one stands at the hinge, crack, or edge between two vastly different modes of being in the world. To awaken *properly, correctly,* it is necessary to know some purpose. There must be a resolve to focus energy and place concentration upon some purpose or action. This resolve can only be effective or true if one considers carefully *before* sleeping the end to which one will awaken.

In the case of the morning run, the resolve must be strong *before sleeping* that one will awaken with the image of the morning run well focused, so that the breathing and tightening of muscles may go on with no thinking save that of resolve to realize the image. (Focus of the image is usually in the forehead!)

ARM MOVEMENTS.

The zen monks of Tibet (Yoga) walk up mountains holding arms straight to sides and with shoulders hunched and fists clenched. This seems to focus energy on the heart-lung system.

Karate moves and thrusts may be accomplished while running. On the expulsion of air with a pushing explosion from the lower abdomen, one may simultaneously throw out the arm chop with hand made rigid by a concentration of energy in the first three fingers, thus putting the edge of the palm and the palm itself in a proper firm tension. Accomplishing this exercise while running is apparently a good means of reducing fatigue of the run.

(The hand tension or rigidity is a difficulty. It is achieved easily enough *at first* by simply crooking thumb, and extending index finger and center finger very hard . . . this makes the hand spontaneously into a tough weapon. But there is a whole world of detail and learning to be experienced in regard to all the varying forms that may be followed just with regard to configurations of the hand. *Transformation* of the hand to a weapon is no less a thing of detail, learning, practice, trial and error, etc., than transformation of the hand into a tool for writing. And as penmanship has an infinite variety of styles and patterns, so too does use of the hand as weapon.)

Small degrees and elements of karate practice, that is, zen forms of combat training, introduce themselves very easily in running. To run is already to be doing the action of a warrior, and it follows that the running praxis is such as to open the body and mind to things of combat: war cries, the expulsion of air explosively from the abdomen, is a natural reflex. Footwork: speeding up, slowing down, side stepping. The arm strokes can fit the rhythm and push-pull of the arms in running. And then a new discovery. One leaps very well and very naturally as one throws an arm or footblow while running. The leap is an easy thing under these conditions, and most important, it seems to rest the body from running even while the running is under way and continuing.

Thus, after some fatigue has set in on the run, one may begin a series of fighting zen actions (e.g., running through an extended grove of trees throwing blows that only touch the bark of the tree trunks) and 20 to 30 seconds of this, or more, has the extraordinary effect of giving rest to the body. One finds a spontaneous means to leap with the throwing of the blows. An accidental discovery: while aiming blows toward passing tree branches one found a need to leap; that is, the body itself leaped of its own accord to better the action, and after a time or two the mind registered this surprising event . . . that leaping was spontaneous, easy, and restful in its effects, when done in accord with the zen principle of *out*breathing (explosive exhalation on leaving the ground).

2 MAKING AN ENTRY WAY

It is now about six weeks since the beginning of these notes. Begun late July, carried to present 1 September. Dating is nonsense by calendar, however. In the beginning it was with great heat and moisture and the earth literally breathing underfoot, and the life of the earth so omnipresent that the breathing in of small insects was a distinct hazard. Now it is already a time of fall rains and chill. Muddiness, puddles in ground and on streets are another kind of hazard and the cloudiness, greyness, is an oppression very different from the hot iron of the sun, yet no less to be mastered if one is to continue.

The change of season reflects the change of meanings that have revealed themselves. Now one has penetrated into the mind-body dialogue sufficiently to see that the mind and body are immensely distant and separate from one another . . . that each has virtually its own life . . . that most typically the mind binds and oppresses the body as the most cruel of masters might bind and oppress his slaves. As the body is given more freedom and allowed to find its way toward its own realization many new horizons open themselves to view. The mind becomes lighter, more powerful, for the burden of maintaining oppression has been lifted from it. There is a cost: the mind cannot indulge itself so easily any more at the expense of the body. Yet as each achieves its own way, the mind and the body grow to be more friendly to one another and move in the harmony of good partnership.

SPIRIT.   The name of the partnership is a third force: "It" . . . "Power" . . . or . . . better perhaps: Spirit. Spirit is apparently quite supernatural in the way it slowly reveals itself. Most important and surprising, it is outside. It is outside both mind and body, seemingly made up of inexplicable happenings. One way it shows is through coincidence. The apparent happening of random events that pile continuously one upon the other until one is literally *compelled* in mind to recognize that the idea of coincidence is finally a greater absurdity than the idea of spirit . . . it . . . power.

One sees it also in forgetting. Forgetting to do things that had been habitual habits of oppression on body by mind. And body's revenge on mind: the physical infirmities, greediness and incapacities and errors and sloth, these things also seem reduced of their own accord, spontaneously, and without conscious effort.

EMERGING DIALECTICAL SYNTHESIS.   This synthesis is not a simple averaging out of counterforces or objects . . . One sees now by the *outsideness* of the spirit that synthesis yields something entirely new and unexpected . . . It is a cardinal principle . . . revealed in the very nature of an altered state of being in the world via the praxis of dialectical running, that what emerges can no more be foretold than the outcome of an LSD trip or a rolling of the I Ching coins (rolling because they are truly dice although most are taken in by the illusion of the coins).

Dialecticians thus share with zen masters a truth that is always completely baffling to outsiders. Namely, that one cannot and should not ever try to anticipate outcomes of correct praxis. One cannot and should not ever say to the apprentice, the neophyte or client, be it person, or institution, or society, that a specific end state or goal can be achieved if . . . "you will only do this and that, thus and so . . ." The end is never reached. And so to posit an end or goal is already to practice deception. Even more, the processes that steady down into describably, *relatively* stable plateaus of being in the world are taken by the naive to be an end state but are only transient points that serve as markers of central tendencies in the variabilities of process.

Q. How fast can you run a mile?

A. I don't know . . . sometimes it is more and sometimes it is less. What does it matter to you? Why
ask a false question?

Q. How fast did you run a mile the last time you
measured?

A. That is a proper question and may be correctly
answered, as, for example, what was the quality of
your last bowel movement? Questions follow from
questions and so we can move toward whatever
truth generates the questions, and know something finally of which we can agree . . . "yes, that
is so . . ."

EVIDENCE OF KNOWING.   There must also be noted what is most prominent in the evidence validating these truths that come along in such surprising ways. When a good truth arrives, one knows it by the blissful joy that comes with it. One feels the pure and simple delight of a child discovering unexpected gifts on Christmas morning. One laughs aloud and tingles, relishing the beauty and strength given in that new truth, and one knows, therefore, without doubt and beyond cynicism or uncertainty, that another pearl has been formed as surrounding pressures have worked upon the seed-grain of correct praxis. This is probably what the philosophers have in mind when they distinguish *knowing* (gnosis) from "mere" knowledge.

LIGHT RUNNING.   The layoff. Dialectical philosophy makes the negation of any affirmation a key to further investigation and understanding of the affirmation. By laying off; holding back to do a light run of about half the usual duration, one negates, and further knowledge is revealed. In this instance, it is the zen karate pull-back or retreat principle . . . balance is achieved via the pull-back. The meaning of the forward thrust is in its retraction as well as extension. So in running, the layoff reveals how far one has progressed both in physical and mental terms. Spiritual oneness of mind and body is laid out more in the open through deliberate retreat from the maximum or extended run, to the lesser, easier run. But this is in itself an effort; one requires a new kind of energy focus in order to stop or hold back when the body is rather eager to go on. It seems fundamentally wrong to hold back from what *can* be done. Why? Maximum achievement is being contradicted. Yet is it not true that the hold-back involves an exercise of power of no less significance than the push forward to furthest limits?

The power of restraint is thus revealed. Restraint is a form of power because it requires control, and power lies in the ability of control.

HARSH WEATHER RUNNING. Wind, rain, cold, create slowing conditions of distraction, mud and slipperiness. Energy must be directed to maintenance of the will to run; to resistance against these new factors that complicate the running.

BREATHING IS CENTRAL. All the zen authorities emphasize correct breathing as the core of the correct praxis, and this is gradually revealing itself to be true in a number of unexpected ways. Thus swimming: without any particular plan or intention, zen breathing simply emerged during a recent distance swim. The startling result was that as the breathing rhythm began to root itself into the activity, one began to accelerate the swimming strokes without the usual sense of exertion or effort. The breathing "lifted" the arms without conscious energy investments. Concentration on the breathing seemed to leave the body free to operate with more strength and lightness in the water. Arm and leg rhythms moved easily and without special exertion into harmony with the pace of the breathing. Rapid expulsion of air through the mouth gave greater force to the arm movements just as it seems to do to the thrust of blows released in time to the release of air. One had for a surprising few minutes almost a sense of attacking the water. This is analogous to the spontaneous feeling of power and aggression that comes with the exercise of such breathing during running.

The dialectical nature of the breathing technique is very conspicuous in the general range of effects that can be identified. Swimming is only one of several examples. What is happening is a new emerging synthesis. By conduct of the zen breathing one necessarily changes other conduct (the interpenetration principle). New, unexpected senses of the body are gained. The body demands rather different, better treatment, and the mind seems to acquire a sharper edge, a brighter clarity. Antitheses are also felt, of course . . . occasional moments of confusion, of not knowing the whys and wherefores of some routine activities that have not been questioned ever before.

Breathing and what comes with it grows stronger as a dialectical force; a center of pressure exerting structural change in the mind, the body, and the dialogue between them.

NOT RUNNING.   The first noticeable effect of not running for a couple of days is failure to maintain focus and concentration on the fundamentals. Breathing is more difficult to concentrate upon; it is not felt as being so essentially the center of being. Why? Because by not running, one has not accomplished the praxis required for pursuing knowledge of being in the world.

Being in the world is easy to ignore, or to bypass, or forget, when there is no strong reminder . . . such as the running. Why does the running work so well as a "spiritual" reminder?

Focus . . . ritual, intention, purpose . . . concentration of energy, revelation of truth in consequence of the thing done. Running demands breathing and breathing forces awareness of the simple fundamentals that are the essence of zen and dialectics.

RUN OF THE DRAGON, RUN OF THE CRANE.   Following zen practice of literal and metaphoric identification of states of being with animals, it is proper to express the discovery of different modes of running in this form. The run of the dragon is aggressive; when doing the zen combat breathing, one comes quickly to a palpable aggressive posture and feeling. Combat breathing, and forming the hand sword, focuses energy in aggressive ways and from this comes rather quickly the feeling of fighting power . . . indeed even a bit of a thirst for fighting, for there is a sense of great strength, invincibility.

The run of the crane is grace. Here the breathing is as smooth and regular as possible, and the body is configured for long, light strides. There is the feeling of freedom and delicacy throughout legs, arms and mind. The image arises quite naturally of the crane, whereas in the former instance with body configured for combat the image is of a fire-blowing dragon.

RUNNING AS ZEN PRAXIS.   The practice of living for zen adepts in the Orient requires simplicity, physical and menial work, and spartan personal habits. By imposing a hard regime of the body zen opens and focuses the mind. Running is especially well-suited to perform this function for people in the West. Just as in the old zen monasteries, the modern runner in the West may be led to a proper state of humility through the menial effort he requires of himself. That is, although running may have an initial effect seemingly contrary to the humbling functions of zen labor, its dialectic is so powerful that no sincere runner can fail to achieve the beginnings of enlightenment.

Thus, no matter how strong and proficient the runner, his strength and skill are limited by the simple realities of time and space. Let him only be required to run long enough and hard enough, and even the world's most celebrated medal winning track star will be brought to a state of rubber-legged exhaustion, and in this state his running can be exceeded by the merest child.

The dialectic of running: if you run enough, your ability to **run** is negated. Egotism blocking the ways toward genuine wisdom can thereby be removed.

In the old zen praxis, steady conduct of hard physical labor and menial tasks was aimed at removing the hard outer layers of egotism blocking entry of direct experience to the deepest reaches of mind.

Running in the zen way can have similar opening-up effects

that carry the runner past thoughts of accomplishment, competition or any elitist sense of superiority. One cannot feel any of these false thoughts if one is truly concentrating on the breathing and stepping rhythms, and on the dialectical connections or unities between mind and the various body parts.

THINKING IN RUNNING.
Concentration upon a koan is the mental equivalent of hard labor of the body. There is no room for intellectual egotism while struggling with what seems an important oracular riddle or parable.

In running there should be at first only space in the mind for the actions at hand: the ground being run upon, and the body praxis needed for the run. Then gradually as skill is achieved, rather than the ego trips of mind such as thoughts of speed, superiority or merit, it becomes possible to fill the spaces of thought with fundamentals. Pure experienced feeling of images concerning real being. To image the crane or the dragon is already a first opening to zen wisdom, for such images while running are, or should be, an immediate aid to the action of running. And so one may begin to see in even this small way how thought can be put in its place . . . as an adjunctive aspect of being. What we generally suffer from is only seeing it the other way around.

The pain and disruption of a twisted foot or ankle if the foot is placed badly on the ground, is a zen gift. It wipes the mental slate clean for some moments and therefore points a way toward pure experience of the human condition.

BREATHING AGAIN.
Breathing seems steadily to open up again after one thought it was closed; after one thought that everything important about it had been clear. What folly! What arrogance! Of course, nothing is ever clear. Or, if it is clear, it may only be so for a short time because all things are always changing. It is only the speed of the change that varies in different things, and even this is no more than a trick of our perception . . . scaling duration or being in space according to a stupid chopping-up machine called a watch or clock. It is quite *arbitrary* to say that a stone ages more slowly than a man.

So yet new things in breathing. The rhythm . . . incredible. It can take over the body. First sign: open and close one hand in rhythm to exhale (open) and inhale (close). Then after a bit the zen experience comes . . . is the hand making the breathing or is the breathing making the hand? And the hand and the breathing then become such a focus as to begin to absorb the legs. One must try to build the rhythm to the point of enclosing everything. It is a form of mastery if possible. And if it is achieved one might then speak of the running as almost self-contained, a bubble of pure experience that should open one to many many new things.

Dialectic: contradiction is indicated by the simple difficulty of achieving handflex-breathing harmony. The larger unity getting revealed here has to do with the extraordinary divisions within ourselves and about ourselves. The difficulty of coordinating the handflex-breathing actions is dramatic evidence of how real our "division of labor" is at the level of the body.

ZAZEN BREATHING IN RUNNING.   Having begun to probe the zen meditation process known as zazen, one discovers that the first step is breathing: counting each breath; moving it down into the lower abdomen and bringing it out again, while concentrating all attention upon this very simple act. The beginning meditator in zen does this until some sense of unity and quiet calm is achieved at will by uniting conscious thought (counting) with what is usually unconscious body activity (breathing). In running this counting exercise is at first very demanding and hard to maintain. The one through ten sequence slips away and gets lost before it can be completed. But when it is completed, or steadily worked upon, the effect is to calm and strengthen the entire body during the run. By doing such zazen breathing while running, the running gets much easier, and even begins to recede: is one running to breathe or breathing to run? Which one makes the other? The questions are clearly spurious for it may be realized that here a true synthesis occurs.

3 DIGRESSION: FEAR AND HARMONY ON A HONDA 350

Nov. 1, '74
COLD, 40'S AND LOW 50'S.   My first long-range ride.
Distance on the odometer: 183 going; 180 coming back (took a
shorter, older road on the latter). Time: about four hours each way.
Average speed: about 55. The wind and cold held it down, but I
wouldn't have cruised over 60 in any case because of my fear of
of straining the machine . . . plugs, points, etc., had not been
touched in 1,000 miles before this trip, and a breakdown on rather
remote roads intimidates me.

First learning: Pirsig is correct. To do this in future, I must
know more about maintenance. My fear on hearing what may
seem like a missed beat of the motor can only be exorcized by
mechanical knowledge regarding points and plug wires and carb
checking.

There is also the business of the chain; something of a
mystique. Every serious rider seems to think of his chain dif-

ferently. How frequently they lube it; *how* they lube it (carefully and slowly between each link or more grossly?) and most of all, how tight they keep it.

When I checked the chain after getting to P-ville, I was amazed. Instead of loosening up as I expected it would after 180 miles of some bumpiness (Highway 24 mostly; a road of the 1930's at least), it was tight. So tight that the rear wheel would hardly turn in neutral when I tested it! First thought was to go to work with the wrench and adjust the chain tensioning bolts. Loosen that dangerous tightness up. Too tight a chain will break. Breaking a chain while at any speed is much to be feared since it is liable to lock the rear wheel, jam in the axle or who knows what. Riders don't talk much about this and they suspicion different types of harsh consequences. Love your chain or it could get you, brother.

So I went over to the motel and got out tools and thought about it. And in getting out the tools I had to get out my lube spray and so I thought first lube it. Bet that's it. True. I had sprayed about half the chain with care when the wheel began to turn more easily and as if by magic, there had begun to return the ½ inch chain slack I am persuaded is correct. (My persuasion to a relatively tight chain is owed to a mechanic in Boulder who was of real charisma in the way he worked and spoke, and told me about keeping such a tightness and lubing a lot, after every tank of gas.)

The ride itself was superb; an ideal two-lane blacktop, that used to be the main route east-west back in the thirties or maybe the twenties. Old gas stations with friendly old guys puttering around in back somewhere. Totally plugged into the machine, watching the rpm's, the scenery, the road of course for mud, sand or farm truck-tractor droppings, and always the beat and the vibe of the motor. The old-time biplane pilots must have become a part of their engines this way. The bike as a whole becomes a part of one's body. The right hand forever glued to the throttle with all the rest free to vary within small limits. On the way back it was very cold, despite four layers of shirts and a warm ski jacket, gloves, helmet, goggles, etc., and even the skier's overpants (wind pants, like chaps). Knees suffer the most out in the wind. Reasonably good chest-head protection from the light wind screen, however, when I scrunched up so close that I was almost touching it with my head.

I nursed the bike most of the way at 50 to 60. For a while near the end it was like being detached in the brain; watching my hands on the grips and the road through the screen like there was a film camera in my head:

> "Head director: pan over right there and get me a close-up of the shoulder going by, keep focused on the shadow of the bike riding the shoulder. Not too long! Cut back to the road ahead and the dark spots; tar? Yes. Swing up and get the hawk perched on the telephone pole, zoom in on rpm dial; you are slowing on this hill; squeeze it a little." Fantastic; another life out of time and all the other.

Think of Lindbergh and one knows why he called his plane and himself "We."

Cold makes it hard to concentrate easily on the riding. My nose drips, and I have to carefully take the left gloved hand up to it, blow into the glove. (I have a bandanna for this but it's in a zipped jacket pocket and I don't want to go through all that to get it and then risk dumping change or other stuff out of the pocket as the bandanna comes out. So blow in the glove and wipe it on the leg of the wind pants.) And if there should be any kind of serious bump, wind gust, big truck from the other direction making sudden suction, or car passing from the back while there is only the right hand holding the steering, it could be bad. So constant running of nose and wiping thereof is no small thing. One is a little out of balance, out of harmony with the machine in order to blow the nose and, thus, closer to danger.

Hawking and spitting is much easier you would think. But to spit the head must be turned over the shoulder to the rear. With strong winds as I had, any quick turn of the head changes the air flow and makes you lean some so the whole bike-rider capsule is affected in its balance. The suction is such that if the spitting isn't done right it can blow back in your face, smear the goggles some.

The sense of harmony and oneness with the machine and the road is the big thing, of course. The harmony is so precise and delicate that even spitting disrupts it. This is a zazen doing! A state of meditation, of getting out of it and into touch with the very small things we usually overlook, is it not? Zen was helpful on the trip. Shivering spasms could be handled with some good slow deep breathing. Also fears of all kinds. My goggles were pretty loose going out, and the first big truck suction wave almost twisted them off, jiggling my glasses underneath as the bike leaned hard. It makes fear but the zen cleared it very well, as it also did the fear of being all alone in remote roads miles from any town or house in the morning cold out on the prairieland. The aloneness is total. A strange meditating loneliness out there. Being part of the machine at 60 mph in cold winds, holding your life in your hands, and the sound of the motor is the only thing that gives comfort, power: if it's o.k., I'm o.k. But it's awfully small and fragile (four cylinders would be so much better than two . . . no wonder Lindbergh was strange after doing this over the ocean).

To run is to learn the body dialectically; all the interconnections ordinarily overlooked. To ride like this is to gain a dialectical feeling for the machine that is almost identical.

4 DIALOGUING THE COLD: QUESTIONS AND ANSWERS

Nov. 18, '74

How is one to understand the extraordinary and almost literal "lift" one receives from a new pair of running shoes (not ordinary, mind you, but Onitsuka Tigers) that confer a springiness, a balance and pitch to the footsteps of running that is new and quite delightful?

Building resolve translates now into felt energy tension. Resolve comes with much greater ease and more force than before.

Looking sidelong from the corners of the eyes is a great aid in meditation or in turning off the mind . . . stopping the internal dialogue and flow of words, worries, and up-down emotions.

Eyes: Gazing ahead, to a point a little below the horizon while running, trains the eyes to scan a wider field. Is this liberation of the eyes?

Running as it gets colder and colder in winter is increasingly dialectical: it imposes a new dialogue with the body via a much closer attention to clothing, and to the practices to be followed after the run.

BREATHING AGAIN.   The zen breathing and midsection exercises not only aid running but also have a wonderfully calming effect on the emotions. This seems very relevant to Don Juan's idea that fear and threat enter one through the lower abdominal area; the "gap." This seems quite true, because the onset of any real fear is literally felt via an emptiness and shivering sensation in the stomach, from groin to belly button.

RESOLVE NEGATION.   Having built a strong resolve toward the action of running, as from the night before setting the time for awakening, and then doing this well, getting up with a direct thrust toward the run, and then *not doing it.* Is this a failure or a transcendence? To know that it is there ready to be done and that it can be done and yet not doing it . . . is it weakness or a form of superiority? Negating a negation of the usual indolence? Or falling back into it even at the moment one is ready to go beyond it?

PREMONITIONS TRUE AND FALSE.   The false premonition is the one that is preceded by an elaboration of hypothetical happenings. One may create fear by running a scenario in the head that leads to a plausible vision of the feared events. The genuine premonition must be something in which the sense of fear and wrong events precedes any rational constructions of circumstances.

VISION.   While running in difficulty of any kind; fatigue climbing up hills, for example, or the inexplicable weaknesses that seems to occur spontaneously at odd times, it is a great aid to visualize beyond the present . . . to "see" ahead or think ahead toward the object to be accomplished. This effort is in close parallel to the karate practice of breaking boards with the hand, wherein one "aims" the hand at a point beyond the board. In Castaneda,

Don Juan explains about the seeing of doubles in the same way: one may imagine oneself to be elsewhere. And so back to running, where one can at least easily imagine oneself to be at the top of the hill, or at the end of the run, with the result that immediate hardship is reduced or eliminated.

RESOLVE.   Inexplicable weakness experienced by runners seems to follow from the absence of a proper resolve to run. As the problems of running grow ever greater with the colder weather, the resolve and its associated factors of more careful preparation stand out as a necessary prerequisite. The unexpected result of this heavier attention to resolve is the relative absence of inexplicable weakness.

What is the resolve? Rather like the commonplace idea of athletes who speak of psyching themselves up, but different in many essentials. Good resolve requires no fear, no hatred for an opponent, no desperation to succeed at any price, no egomaniacal determination to go beyond prior limits established in relation to a stopwatch, and no sense of public performance or impressing an audience. Instead, it is deeply personal, a going out of the mind and into the body.

In zen terms, the run is already accomplished by the preparation of good resolve which can be felt by the gradual accumulation of body tension toward the run. Thinking of the run as physical preparations for it are made, the hands and fingers may be tensed and a tingling of energy felt. Some good breathing and stomach movements will come spontaneously, and in moving about one begins to be automatically on the balls of the feet. To awaken and lie still, summoning up the image of running, is to initiate an almost automatic, reflexive tension that goes to work almost immediately on the body. Fatigue and the soft, dragged-out confusion of ordinary awakenings are simply bypassed. Metaphorically, at least, one who follows this practice is like the matador on the day of the bullfight. It is, in general, what Don Juan would call the warrior's way.

DEEP COLD.   Running in the deep cold (20 or less degrees) is a new thing in itself. A special discipline is required, as it is for ordinary cold; yet something more, because deep cold forces qualitative change. Breathing through the nose only works well if proper grease is applied to keep the dripping from causing sores.

The nose-soreness and dripping require explanation. The more cold, the more dripping; that's basic. What happens is that the dripping needs to be blown out and wiped, not for aesthetic reasons but in order to keep the passages open for easy breathing. So! It is the wiping that makes the trouble; that friction is enough to start sores going as it must be repeated so often, especially at the outset of the run. Now it may well be that to run well enough and long enough would be to reduce this problem to something trivial. This is a thing to be explored. Can one achieve such a correct balance of body functioning in running (like an aircraft or sailboat perfectly trimmed for "hands off" cruising) that even the nose dripping is assimilated to the larger unity and thus obviated?

The wind is the heavier threat, however. Deep cold without wind is like a paper tiger. The wind really does the serious work against running. It requires so much energy and attention to defending against it that one's running is substantially slowed . . . if that is important. How? Well it gets you in all your openings. The ears may be covered by a head band or hood, but unless also stuffed a bit with cotton or paper the wind blows right through into the ear. It can be almost like a cold ice pick probing in there, particularly if one has the wind broadside. Then there are the eyes.

The wind, I mean a good wind at least 20 or 30 mph or gusting to that much, gets at the corners of the eyes even if one is wearing glasses. One feels himself being literally damaged in this way. The wind is our worst adversary; it can eat us up bit by bit, erode the body, maybe, as it erodes mountains.

RUNNING IN A NEW PLACE.   To be in a strange place, country or city, and run in it for the first time is instructive of the strength required for dealing with novelty. One cannot run as freely in the interior, spiritual fashion, because so much attention must be directed outward toward the terrain, the location, and the potential threats that always may be encountered where one has not been before.

5 hARSheR FORCes, STRONGeR hARMONies

Dec. 16

AN OUT-OF-BODY EXPERIENCE. Sudden, unexpected experience of very powerful running without exertion or particular volition. To forget somehow the intentionality of running in this unique (late afternoon, rather tired) situation seems to have liberated an "it" factor; akin to the "it" that Herrigel describes as taking over and shooting the arrow for the zen archer. Powerful long strides up hill and under conditions that have always in the past required the utmost resolve and effort . . . now done easily . . . at least this one time. Maybe some people call this "second wind," but if the phenomenon is indeed coded that way in the "scientific" tradition, that does not influence its validity as an out-of-body sensation; it only shows that we have no serious tradition in Western science for giving meaning to such happenings.

Dec. 18

Another superb morning run; as if the out-of-body experience has left behind a residue of strength and resolution. But now a different and very odd insight; something that might be frightening if it did not come at a time when I feel a sense of strength and control as never before. While closing out the run in a slightly different locale than usual (having decided to go a bit longer in order to peel a shirt and cool before entering the building), I began some hand tensing and tension twisting finger movements . . . the sort I associate with karate, and the other oriental marshal arts exercises. Just then a college girl passed about a dozen feet away, ahead of me. She seemed utterly frail and vulnerable bundled in her heavy coat, and walking head down over books clasped to bosom. And at this very point with my right hand in a quasi sword configuration and the good tension of the run still in my midsection there came this surprising flash thought (image really, too quick for a conscious thought) that this would be so easy to attack; cripple, destroy, or whatever. One's body here suddenly recognized a person as a target, in the same reflexive way as a wolf maybe recognizes a chicken.

A feeling of intense, total power and sudden feral interest in the critter as she passed, and then gone in the surprise of what I had discovered here. A new potential for ferocity growing out of what? The new sensation of strength? Some repressed hostility toward runny-nosed little coeds? None of this! I think it was no more and no less than a sudden triggering of primitive instinct set off by the conditions of the situation. It was an ethology demonstration: that the domineering, aggressive killer instinct is there to be aroused in all of us given the appropriate conditions . . . proof of a kind came as I walked on, rather bewildered but immensely "up," a real high on power, and then round the corner was a small construction job and a couple of guys working on it. One of them looks up toward me and I give him without thinking, a look back which, as I do it, I know is loaded with contemptuous domineering challenge (you wretched human, I'll put your nose on the back of your head) still carrying over from the wolf-like sensation a few moments before.

What is it all about? A feeling of discovery at this new being that can emerge in me. This must be the thing of the dragon; the zen warrior always fights "out-of-body" and "out-of-mind" and one can see this now in a very small tentative way. More important maybe, one sees now what we call schizophrenia. This experience could easily confuse and overwhelm one who was unprepared. It is surely a splitting of the self. Can one break down the previous, painfully built, but obsolete personality integration?

HOW HELPFUL IT IS TO RUN AFTER READING GOOD ZEN.
There is genuine carry-over between the ideas and aesthetics of good zen writing and the efforts one makes toward good zen praxis. In running, there is a notable tendency to slip back toward false daydreaming and familiar, linear thinking, as one goes day after day in the same ways. By reading good zen, the mind is refurbished: furnished again with purpose and the sense of correct action that defines zen. To run after the reading, therefore, is to run with the renewed cleanliness and directness of thought and action which is the fundamental truth of zen. It must be a steady diet of immersion in zen ideas that is required to keep the *dreckerei* down.

One perceives the principle: since the *dreck* is being accumulated inevitably just by the fact of having to be in contact with so much of it, one therefore needs a counterforce. This is, ideally, a true zen master. But failing this, the thing that one has is the writings of zen masters. And these may serve very well indeed.

6 FROM THE OUTSIDE TO THE INSIDE

JAN. 25
WARMTH. It is a warm (42°F.) day of the type called chinook, and to run in this temperature after the sharp-pointed deep cold is like suddenly being on a Florida vacation. There is felt an excess of energy. As the run proceeds to the second mile, after the settling in has occurred, and the zen breathing is strong, the excess of energy seems to provide unexpected strength for acceleration and one moves into the spectrum of super-feelings, feelings analogous to rapture of the deep. It has a certain illusory, deluding falseness, like any "high" as may occur in skiing, motorcycle riding, and upper drugs. Such things are dangerous because they can carry one past the borderline of genuine mind-body harmony into spiritual hubris, where the risk of injury or death is very great because one tends to behave foolishly, without restraint.

Jan. 29
NEGATING THE NEGATION. It has been said by zen masters that one moment is a thousand years, and a thousand years is one moment. In running, one often sees that at the start of the run the end seems infinitely distant, even absurd. (This morning especially, it was grey and cold, 22 degrees. My resolve was very low because of foolish preoccupations with matters that always take care of themselves anyway, and my body was stiff with kinks and dissonant with little pains. I began only with faith in the doing, and even thoughts of cutting short the usual distance.)

RUNNING AT THE TREES (not constantly but every so often) forces the mind away from its false doings. To run at the tree not knowing, and deliberately avoiding, the conscious effort to decide whether one will in the last step go past it to left or right, is excellent praxis because it breaks the linear narrative thinking that can so easily creep into the running effort.

Dec. 24
A TRUE RUN OF THE DRAGON. Up in the dark at 6 a.m.; cold, blowy, and small patches of blown snow spotting the ground. Everything now done with perfect care. It is cold and blowy so one needs the maximum correct planning to go out. This is a real test of what one has learned about running in deep cold. The sweater, sweatshirt, hooded running jacket, ear headband, gloves, and thin trousers (the body takes well care of itself below the waist). This time also the 10 pound weight belt around the waist . . . and as this goes on I have the image from *The Godfather* of the old-time hoodlum belting on his heavy bulletproof vest (they get him anyhow using a garrote . . . when you're hot you're hot).

Putting this on is clearly a dragon act not a crane act; and so is the whole business; cranes stay home under these conditions.

So the run: it is superb; entirely anticlimactic because everything works beautifully. The grease is just right around the nose and mouth. The ears are perfectly protected by the headband and hood, and the hood is cut large enough to give good protection to the corners of the eyes that are not covered by the glasses. The hands are warm in medium gloves, and as usual after the initial chilliness of the first quarter mile, a good warmth and sweatiness comes by ¾ mile, and I end a bit later removing the gloves (grasping them in a fist keeps the fingers warm enough and helps reduce sweating), and loosening the hood.

Running is perfect; this can't be stressed enough. Despite the hits from chilling wind gusts every so often, despite the darkness and shadows of streetlights . . . especially to be careful of when running cracked and tilted sidewalk sections, and very tricky in the trees that cover sections of the park, obscuring branches that can whip across the face and even more tricky, the little holes and depressions that so easily can take you down . . . so, despite all this, the run went superbly well. Excellent strides and breathing deeply to the furthest pit of the stomach.

This is all of great value because it clearly demonstrates that the zen way to running holds up. It has validated itself now in the toughest kind of situation. The run went superbly well because the preparation was superbly done in terms of both the materials and the resolve. Both came together without special, self-conscious deliberation, in a way that would have been simply impossible for me a year ago. Even the smallest of things that could not be anticipated were handled easily. (Thus, avoiding the holes and branches with dodging moves of the running back in football is already a cinch and not notable. But when a car passed the park with high beams on that blinded me, it came almost immediately that one had simply to turn the head to the side and see the way ahead through the corner of one eye.) The strangest thing of all was to discover later, after the run and the shower, that the outside temperature was 23 degrees. Twenty-three degrees and mastered without a flaw! What other personal miracles are there?

COOLING OUT.   The cooling-out period is important. So far overlooked; left to its own devices so to speak, I see now that the immediate aftermath of the run can be of crucial import. While cooling out (coming down in the body and the mind), it is immensely useful to practice movements with great meditative care, and to be aware of the silence and emptiness. A minute or two of still standing now . . . during a pause while toweling off . . .

puts a great quietness into the mind-body harmony one may call spirit.

It begins to be clear that the time after the run, let us say the time of meditative cooling out, is as important as the building of resolve prior to the run. What an obvious and simple truth: that the run will yield its fullest refreshment, composure and clearness of mind (harmony and grace) when the transition period is carried through with some concentration and care, rather than the usual helter-skelter rush to shower, powder and beat the body back into the assembly line doings of everyday life. The point, of course, is to see the run as the spiritual exercise that carries one beyond this stupidity. It is a state of being beyond *while* running, of course, but it is only just now, finally, that enlightenment comes on how the spiritual value of the run may carry over beyond it, if one nurtures a proper zen spirit during the coming-down period. Perhaps I am seeing this because my running is so much better, or is it that by reading more zen this helps the running and in turn helps one to see further meaning and extended value in the entire running praxis? The sense of genuine knowledge gained in these ways is quite extraordinary because it always comes in flashes, and with total conviction. *That* is a true learning.

By the end of the run all was transformed; the distance seemed almost too short, too trivial. It seemed only moments between the start and the end. There was no stiffness, no pain, and no thought that anyone could possibly want to do anything other than this. Here is the magic of zen revealed! It is change and transformation through and with time that allow one to master time by movement through space. One masters the ordinary fears and hurts of time by going into harmonious partnership with it . . . in this instance by running (meditatively, of course, in the zen dialectical spirit). The dialectics here should also be very plain. Could there ever be a better, more concrete example of negative dialectics (viz: negating the negation) than as it occurs with respect to time, distance, and the feelings of one's own body?

ZAZEN MEDITATION. The traditional "just sitting" allows similar understanding or enlightenments. But I can only approximate this under special circumstances. Example: recently in a small bus going from Detroit airport to Ann Arbor (undoubt-edly a classic journey, prototypical in the lives of so many American scholars). Through an effort toward zazen while sitting in that bus I reached an inner core of enlightenment marked by a deep quiet contented feeling that expressed itself verbally in my mind through the steady, powerful thought that it is all merely a matter of molecules in combination: me, the others in the bus, the bus, the road, the planes and all of it. One may feel oneself in the continuous flow of molecules by just sitting.

And what is the result of such experiences?

"Does one do differently after moments of enlighten-ment, master?"
"Yes."
"How?"
"In many ways."
"Tell me one way, master."
"I give more time and effort to the preparation of food."

FEB. 9
CONFUSION.   A run in deep cold this morning; 12 degrees. Following the usual procedure for such conditions, it went beau-tifully. By the end it seemed, as more and more usual now, to be very little. It may become necessary soon to extend range beyond the conventional three miles. Concentration of thought on the run was difficult because of anxieties for a friend visiting unexpectedly from another state. He is in some trouble with his life and this could not be put easily out of mind during running. It is instructive, however, to see that the mind is susceptible to confu-sions and speculative, delusional thoughts when the conventional social self is aroused by the plight of a friend, even when one knows the issue is completely beyond one's own influence. Such is the power of false patterns of thinking . . . or thinking itself . . . as if the imagining of problem solutions for self or another could have any significance other than momentary coddling of that greedy social self.

FEB. 10

FAILURE.   It is necessary now to mention failure and defeat. Today, very clearly, I began by failing to maintain resolve to make the early morning run. I was up a bit too early, and then a bit too late, which is a problem in itself: The unenlightened reaches of the mind always make themselves felt in odd ways . . . like living near an uncertain frontier forest full of wild Indians. Then I further tricked myself with self-indulgence. One knee has been giving twinges lately; fairly strong pain two nights ago. And so in addition to having the small lateness as an excuse (it could have been done despite the short lateness) I also had the knee, and the thought of giving it some extra rest. To run very early, and with extra weight belted on, in the dark and cold would surely put more strain on that knee than the ordinary run. So it went, and I failed to see my loss right there. I was failing to assert my resolve by yielding to the conventional pleas for indulgence, for a retreat or pause in the life and death struggle one wages here against the false constraints of conventional living routines. One must be able to operate regularly and comfortably in the absurd . . . in that domain ruled out of ordinary consciousness by its *apparent* hardship and absurdity.

Defeat too, on this day. Because of the cold (15 degrees and high gusty winds, the latter being the worst of it) I was fearful and put on a too-tight and too-heavy extra sweater. In the running there was, consequently, too much constraint of the whole upper body, and the passage from too much cold to too much heat occurred much more rapidly than it should under properly organized conditions of preparation. There was no intermediate zone between coldness and excessive sweating as there is when the correct clothes are worn. Thus: with much buffeting from the head wind and side wind gusts; too much sweat; cold impacting around the eyeballs; and tight chafing of the upper body; I quit after about the first warm-up mile. Terribly conscious as I did so of having been defeated by my inadequacy. A battle lost. A retreat.

Those who walk on a tightrope with no net below them cannot allow themselves a day off. No distractions or indulgences. Somehow I know that on this occasion the body and the mind combined to defeat the higher unity of spirit. No harmony was achieved.

Feb. 12
CONTAMINATION.   A fair run this morning. Twenty-five degrees, rather cloudy, but no wind to speak of. In general, easy and smooth, but there was a difficulty of concentration such that the mind could not achieve what has been experienced many times already as the higher level of unity with body. Why? One must question the experience, for experience is the only master we have when there is no master. Having come to understand this principle very well through recent travels and skiing, it is possible to use it.

The answer to "why" is quickly attained. Last night was spent attending a basketball exhibition of the Globetrotters. The children were delighted with the crowd, the various acts of the players, the brassy band music aimed at stirring handclapping fervor. In brief: the carnival atmosphere. This is all very hard to bear, for in such mass activities one sees the human condition too clearly. Like staring at the sun with no filtering glasses or other protection for the eyes. But the zen way allows such sad horrors to be borne. In the detachment, however, the children grew also detached for they were one with the crowd, and when it was over they showed an awareness of my indifference, or better, my contempt and sadness at this spectacle. (The players for example: skilled beautiful athletes performing as clowns to please the crowd. What a corruption of their inner core purity to be selling themselves in this fashion. The old vaudeville juggler-acrobat who went on between the halves was much more to be respected; his work compelled more respectful attention.)

Thus, another instruction from the master called experience. Having partaken of a terribly contaminated experience, one is, inevitably, contaminated. And in consequence, the mind-body harmony necessary for achievement of a clean spiritual level of being is impeded. Having been immersed in discord *because of the vulnerability created by attachment to the children,* that discord penetrates deeply enough to prevent the more complete harmony one may reach in zen/dialectical running. What needs to be done is a more intense effort. Tomorrow the early morning run with the extra weight: another day, another lifetime.

7 CLEANSING DIALOGUES OF MIND AND BODY

BODY CLEANING MIND. Having set out to note the contents of the mind . . . what is going on in there . . . what topics, what processes of thought having what aims or meanings . . . indeed, everything that serves as the "contents of mind" one confronts the first barrier which defeats those who cannot gain release from traditional western-linear-science-(Positivist)-logic. Namely, *the intention to note the contents of the mind itself becomes the content of mind.*

This first barrier of linear logic is completely reduced and irrelevant when mind is finally approached in the zen/dialectical way. "To know the body truly is to know the mind; to know the mind truly is to know the body." It has become so in my experience. By running in the correct way the mastery of body gained, be it ever so small, slowly has become a mastery of mind, and vice versa. The ways this kind of dialectical process works to support and enhance both the running itself and the resolve to run; and more and more important lately, also the doings in other spheres of existence—all this has been mentioned earlier and will be again.

This day, however, the noting of mind contents has finally emerged clearly from earlier efforts to simply *eliminate* mind contents. The zazen purpose of "stopping the mind" from its constant flow of content which serves to maintain a continuous but artificial definition of the world (and the reality of one's experience in it) is, in fact, only a first step.

The second step is becoming aware of what those constantly flowing contents are. They are invariably very simple matters or themes. The first theme is *protection;* the mind generates contents serving to protect against the disturbance of mind, self, social being and emotional being. Second is *fame* . . . enhancement of social and emotional being in whatever forms have been dictated by outside forces. There is then *gain;* all the material, as well as social and emotional gains that one associates with fame. There are reflections, memories of the past; there are speculations, hopes and dreams and imaginings of the future. All of these—past and future—involve protection, fame and gain projected backward or forward.

To know this well is to have a new, second grip on the rock face of enlightenment.

To know this well is to realize that, with some notable exceptions, one lives in a constantly self-generated dung-heap of disgusting egotism . . . venial, petty, indulgent, greedy. (Freud knew it well: the more-or-less laundered and sanitized dung-heap called ego or consciousness, constantly being burdened with new *dreck* from id and superego, which steadily generate the garbage that has been programmed in.)

The exceptions: art, at least good art either produced or consumed. Danger; within the limits of edification. Perhaps some philosophy; perhaps some moments of love.

FEB. 21
MIND CLEANING BODY.   The dialectics of zen and the zen in dialectics: always so impressive as they may be seen together

in running. After several days mixed, indifferent, and ineffective running because of heavy snowfall requiring hiking boots and unaccustomed muscle action to lift clear of snow, ice, tire tracks, footprints, etc., it was possible today to return to the regular pattern.

And behold it! The knees and calf muscles make some complaint; there is reluctance and general creakiness through the ramshackle structure; a pull at the groin; a pinch at the ribs; the ten thousand small disgusts of decay, one might say. Even contact with the earth is rough and bumpy; the feet jar on landing . . . the skeleton gives a bit of a shake . . . the organs hanging inside are jolted instead of being nicely massaged . . . and all this accumulates toward a quick production of contamination of resolve, meaning no good harmony and no rhythm nor music.

But one has learned much about these things and how they may be worked upon and assimilated. So it is easy; not to panic, simply back to a more careful, less awkwardly hurried pace, and most obviously, back to a counting of breathing; correct praxis. Then after a time, all is rearranged back into the now-familiar harmony. By the end of the run one is fully recovered.

This is dialectics in action. Always the necessity for a re-creation and renewal. Nothing lasts without receiving its due attention. The great objects of manifest significance distract from the correct praxis of the small things that are the foundation of everything. Thus wisdom is always correct breathing, and correct breathing is always wisdom. There is not one without the other, and without both there is no path beyond the poisons of decay.

Feb. 28
EFFECTS OF SPRING. Clear and perfectly sunny this morning; 31 degrees a bit after dawn, no wind at all, only the stillness and light penetration of warmth that opens up spring on the central plains . . . superb, golden moments here . . . the very old but always newly surprising sense of life coming up again. There is much of zen, much of dialectics in this . . . for it is the praxis of running that opens up the awareness of these matters.

To the morning runner, the weather is as important as it was to the early aviators, for the run is quite obviously a flight of adventure, newly engaged each time, and although the physical risk is absent there is in the judgment to run as well as the conduct of running, the analogous risk of failure, disgust, frustration . . . slipping back into the everyday earth of mudcrawling, of fame and gain as some of the masters have said.

But the praxis of running through the winter has brought with it now, the unlooked-for burst of spring, meaning wonder and joy, a thing of childhood which has its value for the man of 43!

In the action, *it* is realized to perfection. The run went as a dream; perfect sense of rhythms, music-interior, breathing a controlled harmony as much or as little as one wants, wonderful light meetings of feet and earth . . . grass . . . cement . . . a little ice here and there, the frost still on the grass, light patterns mixed through all of it giving positive glows; so much strength and energy coming out of the earth and seeming to be absorbed in the body, is it not? No! One understands from the zen dialectics that it is all one. Having become aware through the running praxis one knows it to be unity. Cold and *down* earth-body together in the worst of winter; warm and *up* earth-body together in spring. There is no difference to be concerned with between earth or body when the harmony has been built, or discovered really, because it was always there.

As for the run itself, body action falls far into the background. When everything works so well, then the mind-no-mind being emerges more strongly. One can understand that running might be pursued sufficiently so that in the end it could become redundant and useless. There are glimmers coming along that perhaps, after all, the just sitting of the Asian masters may be the state that ultimately is achieved at the end of the running.

To sit staring at a brick wall, at the sky, trees, and earth, maybe this is just a reduced speed form for the feelings of running?

MAR. 2
TIME AND DISTANCE.   This morning's run extended further than ever before . . . a new increase in range, by perhaps 15 percent of the old range. With longer range comes no different sense of time or fatigue, however. Why? Because it is all the same as standing still? Because to run is to put oneself into a bodily

condition of unusual functioning, higher metabolism, which over time stabilizes and becomes *not* unusual, but just another state of being: the body functioning simply moved up a notch or two beyond what we ordinarily think to be usual. Thus it seems that to extend the range of the run does not extend the length of time one experiences the running state, because the time does not move or change with the distance.

The running therefore appears to slow down time; not unexpected really if one thinks of Einstein's idea of relativity.

One thing requires emphasis: in running one is taking out the garbage of the body, removing poison in much the same way as a sailor bails out his boat. And in running with the mind in a zazen direction, cleared of imaginings and immediate life-scenario contents of fame and gain, there is also some removal of mind garbage. Then comes the best quality experiences of no-time and no-distance.

MAR. 7
KEEPING PROPER AWARENESS.   To have zen running one must have consciousness of zen teachings. The running does not have its extended meaning of holding time and stopping conventional garbage of the mind unless the awareness of zen . . . of meaning beyond meaning or sources of knowledge beyond knowledge . . . is maintained. Going without some study of zen for a few days leads away from it. Even the running becomes inadequate, because with lesser awareness, the running is accompanied more and more by the garbage; the effluvia of mind, fame and gain imaginings, plans, potential manipulations . . . all of the so-called normal flow of consciousness consisting of whys and wherefores that only create illusions and corrupt or entirely eliminate experience of the immediate present.

8 ENTERING SPRINGTIME

MAR. 9

OTHER ZONES. Some light snow and temperature 30 degrees; little wind. A perfect run extended to yet a new and greater range. Yesterday's run with the extra weight seems to make this day's run a very light affair, easily extended through still another grassy park. The point is reached where the run may simply go on with no felt limits or boundaries. One has here the sense of the unlimited run and consequently, the unlimited being; one is centered in one's being as the zen combat masters speak of it.

There is rare pleasure in such running. Music always seems to come through, playing of the body in the mind. Rhythms of the body. Perhaps it is not possible to run in this fashion without having the spontaneous flow of music into the mind as water flows into a well-hole.

Besides the music there is also clarity of thought. If garbage-thought is reduced does this make room for clear thoughts? It would seem so.

The making of such a run is a making of entrance into another zone of being . . . having the music, and turning the head round and about, up and down, also makes pictures. So it is a sound and vision experience as well as thought and body clarity experience. All coming together to be the framework of a beautiful private and free being. When the masters are just sitting, they too are in the other zone, whatever it is for them.

There are other zones available in the actions of all genuine steps beyond artificial programs of mind and body: skiing, motorcycles, tennis.

The free zone of music and pictures, clear thoughts and body rhythms, occurs in the motorcycle through speed, sound, and vibration. The unity with these things making a oneness and a fullness beyond all rationality . . . alen rationality . . . rationality is always alien. Created by others; stuffed into us by others. Painful at first, because we know it is costing us our poetry as it tears down the separations we need for our universality within ourselves, yet like so many painful things (such is the nature of animals) we ultimately grow to like it! It takes something powerful to get past these imposed, alien tastes.

The motorcycle is a powerful clean instrument that can carry us out of those traps our mamas got us into with all their good species group survival intentions. But the cycle is still outside, while the running is inside.

MAR. 19
INSTRUCTION OF PAIN.   Running with the pain of injury, in this case the left side of the lower rib cage bruised from a ski fall, is another experience. It teaches what must be felt by those who are old and infirm . . . fear of pain during simple movements. But it also teaches that one need have no fear, because one can always work around it in practice.

Like holding a bundle of cracked crockery; that is how F. Scott Fitzgerald described his crackup period, and that is the phrase that describes running with bruised ribs. One goes gently, delicately, trying not to shake up the goods. The mind is most interesting under these conditions. Ordinarily, it is like a large dog held on a thin leash of discipline and correct practice, such as counting the breathing. With this steady possibility of rib-pain, however, the mind does not pull very hard. Or perhaps the pain pulls back against it so steadily that it cannot get away so far as it might under regular conditions.

Mar. 21
PAIN-RHYTHM DIALOGUE.   Fifty degrees, sunny, no wind; running through the first day of spring over a medium distance in order to nurse the pain of the bruised ribs. So long as the steps are not jarring and the breathing is not too sharp and deep, the pain is so small as to be unnoticeable. Any deviation, however, and it may come suddenly alive to give a good little bite. Yet the zen way is to work with what is available. The rhythm and moves of running around the pain are very satisfactory. And the spring day is superb for it allows a lightness that cannot be achieved if one is wearing the heavier garments of winter. It also brings heavier sweat . . . much runoff across the brow and toward the eyes . . . the body is the real seasonal thermometer.

Mar. 23
POWER EXPERIENCE.   Sixty-two degrees! Warm and sunny and windless again. It won't last but it is the first real taste of summer . . . enough, despite the residue of injury, to make running a new maximum distance seem little or no change. There also came back this morning the resurgence of power and strength occasionally experienced in earlier runs. That is, while running out-of-self, concentrating on what is outside and particularly upon the shadow of the body, there came a simple, spontaneous thrust to greater speed, power, and lengthening of strides. A mystical form of experience for it seems unpredictable, unplanned, without effort, yet suddenly one goes much faster and easier and even after a few hundred yards there is no need for much heavier breathing. Like all mysteries it is a bit frightening, and one does not push it too far.

Rapture of the deep in running. Not something to be taken lightly.

Mar. 24

NOWNESS.   So much for spring: 30 degrees and extremely high wind gusts this morning, enough to cut right through the high-necked shirt and vest remaining after removing the sweat jacket following the first mile and a half. Yet, for all this, a certain nostalgia and pleasure already in these last dregs of winter. One begins to miss the cold knife blade of icy wind and the pleasure of moving through it. A masochistic joy? More like another instructive internal contradiction. How hard it is to think about what you are doing while you are doing it. Perhaps one way to tame the mind is by asking it frequently, what am I doing *now*!

Mar. 26

ASKING THE MIND.   A slow going, medium range run in the face of 28 degrees and extreme wind gusts. The legs and knees gave some pains; fatigue for some reason. One works through this after the first mile or so, but then with the hostile weather there was only determination, not inspiration. The mind as usual in these conditions always trying to escape and evade; get itself off the leash and into fantasy imaginings, indulgences of fame and gain. There is a new weapon useful in the mind-control struggle, however. One has only to ask the question "what are you doing right now?" to bring thought down to immediacy.

Mar. 27

PLAYING THE MIND.   Grey and cold, 28 degrees. Running over a medium to long range went well. There is some mastery now in maintaining a comfortable accommodation with cold weather. The mind comes more and more to demand attention, however. One realizes how wildly it fluctuates; trying to maintain immediacy of mind directed at the moment of experience is like trying to control a kite in a high wind: there are good enough moments of steadiness showing the possibilities of immediacy, but then it leaps; looping away to the fame and gain, work and play scenarios of past and future. It will not stay long in the present. It bounds from wishing to worrying and back again . . . a Ping-Pong ball in the game played by id and superego. This is becoming the real occupation of zen running.

MAR. 28
REGRESSIONS.   A medium to poor run because of apparent leg fatigue; there was less than the usual lightness and detachment and rhythm. Why? Suspect it is the effect of a bit of sloth. Yesterday was spent poorly; an afternoon and evening of feeding and reading and smoking. Little or no proper mind or body control. The high level of running simply cannot be maintained unless a relatively high and general level of being is followed. Perhaps it is partly a problem of weather. The dullness is now beginning to go as a period of clear and sunny days comes along. The let-down, the sinking into the swamp of mind-body diversion such as feeding and reading for entertainment, which is in fact itself an absurdity (what is "entertainment" if not diversion from simple reality?) will pass as the spring brings a better praxis, higher concentration.

⑨ mYST€RI€S

APR. 1

DOWN AND UP. An extraordinary resurgence! Poor weather and poor running over the past several days, and today in even worse weather, the sense of being in touch with the Big Enchilada, the absolute as they say, One Mind and all that, has come back with great force.

There was resolve building out of these feelings of unsatisfaction and mediocre fatigue . . . a strong conviction growing inside there that something was rotten (or beginning to rot) in the praxis of being, otherwise the retrograde feelings would not have been gaining strength. Resolved then: greater effort! Not to counter sloth of feeding and reading and fame and gain (the **two** generic dimensions) but rather to move affirmatively in some further direction toward zen praxis. Which means, what?

I know that koan: *any* direction away from the garbage is the zen direction . . . maybe into the garbage is away from the garbage sometimes. Whatever one wants in words is no matter. The run today was a thing of utter perfection; just going along with marvelous rhythm and joy and a sense of being at periscope depth after a long time; I could see above the ordinary surface to that perfectly clear, unmarred, just-so-ness they talk about.

APR. 4
SEEING TREES. Continued variation of nature: yesterday running in two inches of snow in many places; today in 45 degrees, clear spring weather and only traces of snow here and there. The running itself is seemingly receding . . . less and less in the foreground even as one does it. Instead, there is now coming in some new contacts with things of the outside. The ground one runs upon, the trees that look on, so to speak. There is some sense of joy . . . peaceful positive satisfaction and reassurance that comes in from trees lately. They have this living quality; they are there, alive and growing, all the time, just being mute witnesses to the whole show. Attending rather more closely to trees now, there comes some grasp of their presence and being, like beginning to smile at understanding of some subtle practical joke. There they are, standing around all the time, living in our eyeballs and nerves (and we perhaps in theirs?), looking marvelously beautiful, moving enough, changing enough, but given no credibility for life. It is plain enough now that when it comes to the trees, the old subject-object patterns cannot be maintained. We are in it together.

APR. 8
ODD VARIATIONS. Yesterday's run was cut short because of heavy rain, and immediately after stopping the run there came a period of dizziness; minor vertigo. This grew more pronounced later in the morning, but had largely disappeared by evening. The run this morning produced no sign of anything unusual. Perhaps the dizziness was a momentary bodily reaction to some activity of the prior day? Yet to all appearances, there was nothing unusual in that prior day. What is one to make of an event such as this? Nothing, as near as can be told; it is just another happening one moves through.

DREAM KNOWLEDGE. Pirsig's discussion of quality appeared during a dream involving someone reading a list of data which had to do with heights and weights of people. They asked why these data were supposed to be important and the answer came that it was a definition of quality. I.e., quality is never inherent in a single variable, but always must be defined by at least two variables, and by the nature of their interaction. In this instance, it seemed very clear that one could define bodily quality as a multiplicative function of height and weight. This may be an important idea; if so, it is the only one that has ever come out in a dream state for me, although I have heard and read of such things happening to others. It is curious that this occurred on the occasion of the vertigo.

Apr. 10
THE TREES CONNECTION. Finally, total change-over into spring. The gloves and ear protecting headband are no longer carried; the running is consistently getting lighter and tighter. Teachings of the masters emphasizing the elimination of conceptual thought can be followed more easily now, maintained for longer periods, and the results as initially experienced are interesting. There is a primacy attached to the outside because of suddenly increased feelings of connection with the outside. Most powerful in connection with trees; it is the equivalent of going from a black-and-white film to color . . . very suddenly the trees are full of meaning . . . there is a sensuous feeling of mutuality with the trees which results in a strong sensation of simple pleasure or joy.

Apr. 17
MIND SLIPPING. The heat of spring is now becoming more regular and intense. To run on a sunny 50-degree morning is to sweat again in ways that require wiping off as one goes. Fatigue seems to grow as a barrier when the sweat increases in this fashion. It is clear that very early morning runs must be utilized more frequently, and that some mid-day activity on the track in shorts is also required. Concentration on the immediate action of running—no thought—has generally been good but seems to vary with

circumstances. Recent sudden burst of heavy work responsibility has been a disturbance. The mind slips away when practical affairs grow dense. Instead of clear calm water it is like a rocky, foamy stream and one can't see through it so easily. Catching the mind is like trying to land a hard fighting trout.

APR. 19
THE PRODUCER. Cecil B. DeMille . . . that's what we have in our heads producing and directing the constant flow of fame and gain scenarios. This morning's run in 45-degree drizzling weather brought with it two curious instructions. The first is best called the DeMille insight. It is to know that what is running through the head are no more than movies; strips of thought and dialogue with no particular reality other than that which the Producer has arranged for a momentary entertainment.

The second instruction was from the legs; they seem fatigued and sources of pain. It may be that the body is beginning to speak up again, perhaps saying that there has been too great an emphasis through these last few months on the discipline of long range runs. It may be that a new and instructive contradiction is emerging via the legs. This will be something to probe further by opening more extended awareness to fatigue and pain while at the same time letting the DeMille strips run their course, with the knowing that behind the screen, so to speak, there is lying the true state of being.

APR. 21
LET-DOWN. Continued decay in the running. A relatively short range run which covered only the standard distance of several months ago. There is a sense of coming down the other side of the mountain in all this. The let-down that follows on achieving the summit.

APR. 25
RENEWAL. An early morning run, finally, and the leg fatigue and dullness it brought with it has disappeared. Here is a true zen/dialectical instruction! Contradiction, the breaking of

routine patterns, is everything. The monotony and routine of running the same routes day after day had apparently accumulated in such a way as to impose the recent pattern of leg fatigue. This judgment came along slowly, just as the fatigue seemed to grow slowly, but the very early run wearing extra weight has this morning resolved all doubt. The run went beautifully; despite the extra weight, it went lightly and with a sense of power that has been largely missing in the routine morning runs of the past several days. So the instruction is very clear. One is back to the matter of resolve, but in a new way: resolve becomes deadened and little more than an awkward tyranny when it is routinized. By taking the very early run this morning all its qualities were changed and a revitalized sense of purpose emerged. A zen saying could be invented here: "that purpose which is no purpose must be steadily renewed."

Apr. 27

INSIGHTS.   One day laid off, and then a regular maximum distance run this morning that went beautifully, albeit soaked in sweat. But my lay-off day was taken for the purpose of re-equipment; complete change of clothing, spare towels, talcum and lotion, all prepared now for the end of the run. The fact is that running in the warm requires just as much preparation as running in the deep cold. One's concentration begins with the preparations. Just as it was necessary very early to learn care and concentration in tying the sneakers, virtually as a ceremony, it is necessary to learn care and concentration—management, actually—in all the other matters of infrastructure supporting the run. To discover what is needed in the way of infrastructure is a task in itself, harder than the actual implementation. It is said by masters of the zen martial arts that a combat is decided before the first blow is ever struck. So it is with the run: concentration, resolve, preparation, and then the running itself is only an after-thought . . . the arrow shoots itself; the runner is propelled by the run.

It may be of some value to note a minor new instruction as well. The sweat that begins to pour down after about the first mile forces removal of eyeglasses. This in turn provides a relatively new perception experience with many satisfying overtones, for one sees the world again with one less conceptual structure in the way. With and without glasses . . . telescope . . . microscope, etc., all different, all conceptual in distinct ways, all teaching that what is outside depends on what we are looking through.

10 NATURE, MIND AND BEING

EXTRAVAGANZA MOVIES.   The early morning runs with extra weight are going beautifully. A different route is available for those runs because there is no appreciable auto traffic, and this change of scene is perhaps also contributing its benefits. The impresario of the mind still operates, but with the change of scene and the dramatic sunrise spectaculars that are so easily viewed in the new scene, the locus of dramatics has shifted more to the outside. This morning, for example, nature produced a shot right out of Hollywood: sunrays very distinctly breaking through a 30 percent cloud cover; it only lacked Heston in the role of God. One may be instructed by such happenings in the self-deceptions the masters speak of when we grow too impressed with the appearance of external events, as well as the internal events. To be boggled by a super-enriched sunrise is only to move our Cecil B. DeMille indulgences to a new location.

May 1
NATURE PLOTS. Circa three miles in an early-early run through a clouded-over morning, with the weight, and nature was very quiet this time; no Technicolor extravaganzas. There was only the greyness and the grass. My early run site is a grassy high school playing field which provides a lush carpet of clumped, relatively high grass. Lovely to go on and provocative because of the hidden little holes here and there that can take one down with a very bad ankle twist. Having had one of these last year in this place, I do not take it for granted anymore.

No small part of the running experience is this general sensitivity to weather and nature-changes and terrain. Also there may be dogs. This morning a large black Labrador, young yet, but with big barks and teeth. He was in very close and I kept telling him not to be afraid, while moving along in the regular pace. The hardest time is when they get behind you and you can't see if they are coming in for a piece of leg or not. One feels more vulnerable these days going in shorts, but there is nothing to do except keep right on with the regular pace and hope for the best. Today it worked fine.

It begins to seem that Henry Thoreau was often deceived by nature. He apparently turned to it the way many youth turn to religion, out of a disgust with humanity and all its faults. But nature is really no different, only more *in*different.

May 4
PERFECT RUN, TRUE MIND. A long-range (ca. 4 miles, for curious posterity) regular morning run today; perfect weather (60 degrees, no wind, clear sky) and a perfect run. To achieve the perfect run is still something that seems mysterious. It began to emerge in the first ⅛ mile perhaps, just as a feeling of power, of *doing it* in the chest and lungs and arms as well as the legs. Also lightness . . . just finger flipping lightness and grace . . . a sense of ballet in all the moves. Then it settles in somewhere in the second mile. A smooth moving along in what seem to be perfect strides; not too long, but longer than usual. And most remarkable, there is no leg pain at all. Some days there is leg pain almost at the

outset and others, like this one, are completely free from any pain. It is certainly a thing of the mind, but which one?

There is now for sure, discovered on this run very clearly and forcefully and even put to minor test, a clear realization of three levels of mentation-perception, as we say in Western science, or three "mind ways" as the masters might say.

The first is the sensory perceivers . . . the direct mind as technical guide, not only allowing sight of pathways, rocks, limbs, obstacles, but also permitting rapid calculation of coping actions. Sound is very strong here too when it comes to automobiles. One begins with much attention to the sensory perceiver technical guidemind.

Then there is the long range calculator and impresario mind. Call it the occasional savior . . . it gives us scientific thought and logic, of course . . . but perhaps better recognize it more frequently as the Great Deceiver . . . it gives the illusions of control, of power, and even, in all humility, the Hollywood of the mind: double and triple features always with the same fame and gain contents.

When technical guidemind is working well in running one hardly pays attention to it . . . thus easily falling prey to the Great Deceiver . . . not to be bored, as the entrepreneurial runners say.

But then there is Mind, true mind, the oceanic, the Mind of the Way. To glimpse this is to have the satori experience according to the masters. In running it is felt as described in earlier notes, perhaps, as oneness with all. The trees tend to stand out for me in this regard as they may be experienced without conception, without ideas in the head. One goes in this way without concepts, without thinking, and with the prior minds turned to zero calibration, or, as happens more frequently, with the prior minds operative merely as shadows . . . vague overlays or dissolve scenes . . . superimposed on Mind.

Today all three were clear, and if not quite mastered, at least easily distinguishable from one another.

Why now? Only two things are different in today's run: wearing of light clothing (shorts and thin shirt: the body relatively unbound, as it were) and a change in praxis over the past several days. Less food intake, plus the early morning runs with weight.

The food matter seems more and more critical. To gain

greater detachment from eating is very basic. It may well be that conventional eating to a criterion of satiation, or close to it, is a narcotic. This at least seems clear for my own praxis. The eating-snacking routines go with meaningless activity of TV or *Time* magazine reading, sloth, fatigue, dullness, and mild amiability of a semi-comatose nature. One begins a new praxis in this regard; clearing away the next level of garbage in being.

MAY 9
MIND-OPENING. A good long morning's run; it seems that the warm weather and consequent sweating provides a lubricant. One is greased along the ways of the run as the sweat begins to pour out in the second mile. At the same time, it forces some confrontation between the different minds discussed earlier. The sensory-perceptual mind of here and now which guides the footsteps, avoids the holes and stares heavily into the bark textures of passing trees comes up against the impresario mind spinning scenarios about fame and gain. And when this happens, as it does increasingly now on the runs, and even occasionally in other circumstances, the result is to open a path toward Mind. The prior two forms of conventional mind cancel each other out and suddenly there is space, freedom, a whole vista of being; what the masters call "suchness."

MAY 15
ENERGY. Very steady, solid zen runs over the past several days, alternating between early mornings with weight and regular mornings over the longer range. This morning it was the latter, and it's quite surprising to note the extent of ease or facility that permeates the running now. One has the sense of having entered into a new season of phase typified by a felt increase of power and control. Is this only due to the regularity of the activity or does it also relate to the new care and attention given to food, namely, eating less? Probably both. The body rhythms in running make themselves felt rather differently lately. One is reminded of the Buddhist notion of energy, called *ki*. They speak of the flow of ki through the body, and its focus on particular parts or limbs during

certain exercises or through acts of will. Today's run conveyed a sense of ki starting as the foot touched the ground and flowing upward and outward through the fingertips of the hand moving in rhythm with the foot. It seemed almost as if the energy entered the foot and then flipped from the fingertips after traveling quickly through the lower body. Welcome ki.

May 19
APPROACHING HORIZON.   There is beginning now a strong sense of having crossed yet another major boundary; the runs having been going so well, with such a sweet solid smoothness and deep satisfaction, that the whole feeling gained is equivalent to what has been said of conversion experiences. Both the early morning runs and the regular runs of distance later in the morning proceed with a harmony and feeling of power that is quite new. More important, the after-periods are more and more pure moments of serenity and joy . . . simple joy of smiles and songs on the inside of the skin. It is harmony and serene joy of "suchness"; of "just being"; and of "unattachment." The unattachment tends also to be growing outward, permeating into other spheres of everyday life, and new worlds of being seem to be coming forward. I could not have believed it possible.

11 CROSSING OVER

Elapsed time since the last notes is very long, and an immense number of things have happened in the interval, many if not all directly relevant to this record. Essential facts: I have driven by car over 3,000 miles; I have ridden a new four-cylinder Honda over 1,000 miles; I have run, and run well in the zen way, in motel areas near the interstate, at over a mile above sea level in Colorado, at sea level along the ocean in New York, and now back in the Great Plains.

The running has now reached a point of both qualitative and quantitative perfection that I did not earlier think possible, and that I realize, even now in saying it, is of course *not* perfection. But it is so according to one's former usage and understanding. The power, strength, command, certitude, conviction, sense of total authenticity and mastery . . . all these and many more adjectives apply, but always with the caveat that these things, even where they sound authoritarian, are not; they are in fact something beyond that, and beyond whatever the liberal opposite of authority is; they are things that proceed from genuine harmony of mind and body. The running now has no specks of garbage on it. I have it now completely as a unitary gestalt. There is no significant thought anymore, and very little need to exert mind control, or exercise power over mind contents, and the reason is that it now all works spontaneously, better than I ever thought it could, although undoubtedly there is still more to come.

In brief, I now know in full truth and rock-hard certainty that I have *passed over;* crossed some sort of rubicon of my life in the running, and in most other ways as well. Although this record is deliberately confined to running, the implications of the zen dialectical way to other aspects of being cannot be ignored. I am sure beyond all doubt now that one cannot truly practice this way of running without re-ordering and re-arranging all other significant aspects of one's being in the world. This is of course not surprising, for it is precisely what all the masters have said of zen ways, whether in archery, meditation, flower arrangement, or martial arts.

This is not a change in personality . . . one's traits, values, attitudes, and essential stylistic patterns are influenced, of course, but that is not the main thing. Indeed, these sorts of changes have occurred but they seem to me to be quite trivial. What is not trivial is the conviction growing—already present in strength—of the "it" beyond personality. One form this takes which is of great significance is the definite reduction of fear and anxiety on the one hand, and the extraordinary increase of energy and focus on the other. The best analogy or example I can think of has to do with "method" acting, in which the actor literally lives his role and finds the means to do so by altering his practice of everyday life, and drawing upon new actions as the inspiration for living the new role. For me, the experience of "passing over" (I hesitate to say satori or enlightenment) is just of this nature. I am the same person, the actor, but I am in a new role. Beyond this, the role is so superb, the doing of it so satisfying and evocative of joy, that I find myself happier (if that word has meaning) and freer and more content than at any other time in my life.

12 EPILOGUE FROM THE OTHER SIDE

JULY 16

This will be the final entry. One knows finally, when any given life action is completed, because the signals of completion are unmistakable. For the running action there has been a full realization of zen-dialectical wisdom achieved over the past weeks. It is possible to run now in ways that were undreamed of before, and without *consciousness* of the mind-body spirit harmonies. No consciousness anymore of the struggle to achieve the harmonies because they are simply present.

The running now is no longer of important instructive value; it has given what it had to give, and now it is all reflexive in the way that driving a car or motorcycle becomes after years of practice.

Breathing in the correct fashion requires no thought; making the perfect steps requires no thought; meditative and aggressive variations of rhythm come in as they are required by circumstance and demand no thought.

Instead of the struggling and thinking discipline (i.e., discipline over thought and bodily action), there is now liberation of spirit in running that occurs immediately and beautifully. Distances, weights, weather conditions, and all the sundry matters of resolve simply take care of themselves now, as does the all-important and central action of breathing. In fact, it is now extremely difficult to create situations that require attention to breathing because it works so well on its own.

And the result? Physically, in ordinary terms, superb. I am about ten pounds lighter, and trimmer throughout the body than ever before. Heart-lung system seems to be of infinite power. More important, however, the spiritual integration of mind-body is, if not fully complete, then more complete than ever seemed conceivable. The passing over to a new plane of living and doing, of praxis, and yet also of thinking, is very definite and very clear. One lives in a new body and with a new spirit, and old faults, stupidities . . . the entire catalogue of self-indulgences promulgated into the psyches of my generation . . . have dropped almost completely away. It is not too much to say that this year's practice of zen dialectical running has made a new person of me; has impacted finally as a kind of total re-birth. In this connection, it should be noted also that my entire personal life structure . . . social living in the world in its most fundamental manifestations . . . has also changed and continues to change very drastically.

At the conscious level of emotions I am struck by one very salient general result: In virtually every facet of living, I now have little or no fear (disturbance, tension or whatnot) compared to what existed earlier. One has, very definitely, and forever, left behind the prison walls of conventional living. And the direct, almost continuously euphoric feeling that has been with me now for weeks, is approximately like that of being discharged from the army . . . but much, much better. The key phrase for the summary of the entire newness being experienced is simple: Free at last.

BOOK TWO
THE SITTING

1 ANOTHER BEGINNING

FEB. 10

Since coming to the end of the year of running, it has become more and more clear that although running would continue to be a fundamental life praxis, it had no important further instruction to offer.

But during the past several months of assimilating the running experiences by working through the notes and continuing the praxis, the knowledge that meditation . . . true meditation in the Buddhist tradition of just sitting . . . could become the next effort has grown increasingly strong. Now it begins. Ten minutes each day, starting today, on a clear morning of spring-like weather that has been absorbed somewhat during a relatively short run. What is felt?

Excitement of stillness . . . given by the awareness of movement all around that is usually ignored, or thought to be stillness, because in comparison to the familiar activities of mind and body, most other things appear to be still. The images one has through the eyes, for example, appear to be in motion. There is a kind of reverberatory movement to them. And one also becomes much more aware of sounds: how rich and diverse are the patterns of sound that reach the ears from the surrounding environment. It seems that as one achieves even a small measure of stillness, the rest of the enveloping world seems to be in a surprising state of activity.

Feb. 13
MECHANICS OF QUIET.   The third day and already
the pattern becomes familiar and feels more directly natural. Place the sitting cushion; take position (a simple cross-legged posture, the lotus I have never achieved yet) and begin, without any particular effort, to count the breathing. Attention to breathing as learned in running now seems reflexive, second nature, as it were, and nothing is more essential, for it is the gateway through which one moves out of the ordinary configurations of everyday activity. Breathing is apparently the first and most important route toward gaining a grasp on mind. It works so well, yet it is so curious that breathing should serve as the primary key to mindfulness.

Feb. 14
Mechanics of meditation seem very simple; one needs a quiet room or place outdoors where disturbances are unlikely. Quiet doesn't mean total silence, of course, for there really are no such places . . . I once saw a young man in the half lotus position meditating at the end of a rock jetty extending into the Atlantic Ocean while waves were breaking loudly on both sides of him. Quiet is not entirely absence of sound; it is the absence of disturbance. Ruptures, clashes, clangs, sudden and staccato shakings and bursts of tension; these produce disturbance, and these are the properties expressed by most people. Natural sounds, the rhythmic activities of nature, tend to make a condition of quietness rather than disturbance.

One also needs a sitting pad or cushion; almost anything will do so long as it provides the minimal comfort required in the cross-legged position. There are great differences to be noted between sitting in an ordinary chair and being in a cross-legged position on the floor. The latter is, at the very least, unusual. It is special. Specific to the act, producing a different feeling of the body, yielding a different system of tensions or forces in the body which may have something to do with the pull of gravity.

Time seems odd in this activity. The first five minutes feels very long . . . like the first half mile or so in running. Then one seems to get deeper in; the time sense recedes and there is a shift into a state of penetration. One penetrates the stillness barrier, perhaps, as jet aircraft penetrate the sound barrier. The second five minutes is much easier, more meaningful than the first. Today I extended to a third five minutes and found nothing that can be put in words, no dramatic sensations or changes, only a continuation of the stillness. Once some concentration is achieved, apparently, extension to longer periods is facilitated. Like running, the more you do, the easier it gets.

Feb. 16
POSITIONS AND PLACES.   Some positions are better than others. Within the basic cross-legged posture, many small variations are possible. This morning it seemed for the first time that as I approached the more classical, upright Buddhist posture, there was an increased sense of focus and genuine mindfulness, or mind control. Slumped into a lesser version of this posture, mind contents were relatively loose, variable, and without sharpness. When the classical pose was achieved toward the end of the period, mind was rather suddenly cleared. The spottiness of the prior several minutes receded.

Yesterday, unexpectedly, while on a family outing, there was time and a suitable place for a first effort at outdoors meditation. It was a warm, windless day. After some moments of just sitting and getting into the lovely scene of water, rocks, and weathered trees through the attention to breathing, I felt deeply immersed in a particular tree form. This went on for some time, seeming more remarkable because of the wide range of sounds and moving objects present (water, floating debris, people and cars in the far distance). The most striking thing of all was to discover late at night, when going to sleep, that I had a perfect eidetic picture of that outdoor scene in my mind. Without particular volition, every detail of the rocks, water and trees was pictured in mind, and I could focus on different portions of the scene just as I had done in the afternoon when moving my head and eyes . . . only now it was like moving a projector in my mind. A bit later, the picture shifted so as to produce a low aerial view of the scene, which now included the cross-legged figure of me sitting on the rock. All of this "recollection" went on with little or no conscious effort. Today, the pictures still are quite fresh, although I expect they will deteriorate over the next several days.

FEB. 18
GOING AND STOPPING.   In running it has seemed that the faster one goes, and the more rapidly the body travels, the slower goes the mind; the more empty and relatively inert it becomes. The difficulty of just sitting is that when the body is very still, the mind tends to become very rapid. Initially, at least, by the action of quieting the body the mind appears to be released—let loose—into quick, jerky actions. Images and thoughts seemingly rush in to fill the emptiness created by the still body. Lacking the customary focus provided by purposive conduct in which both the mind and body are directed to some goal, one is subject in the opening phase of meditation to anarchy of mind: it flows, probes, and explores chaotically over the whole terrain of one's life space.

Awareness of the chaos may be the first step toward the mindfulness discussed by masters of meditation. Many of them speak of the necessity to focus on a single object or thought in order to control the confused mental activity; in some meditation disciplines, chanting Om or repeating a mantra is employed for this purpose. The purest way, however, seems to me to involve immersion in the mind chaos as suggested by some zen masters. Through such immersion there may develop a familiarity with mind that will lead on to the regions of greater depth. At this early stage in the practice, it may be foolish to try to rush too quickly into disciplines for slowing or emptying mind. Instead, one needs to find out about its predilections and accustom oneself to its characteristic patterns. Control, focus, and depth will all begin to emerge in due course if one works at this from the correct foundation. My task for the next weeks is simply building this correct foundation.

2 ONE STEP FORWARD

FEB. 19
MIND CONSTRUCTION. Last night driving alone on the interstate for an hour, I attempted to practice the meditative state insofar as it might be done without risking an accident. The first result was a sense of energy. By switching off the usual run of mind as one had already switched off the car radio, and then immersing into the full sensory experience of driving, eyes wide open and focused out at the limit of the headlights, there came a feeling of unusual energy; a sense of vitality rather than tension.

The second and more impressive result came after about fifteen minutes, with awareness that the focus and concentration was breaking down my orientation to the highway scene. That is, by concentrating in the meditative fashion, the larger sense of the highway began to disappear. It was like looking into a static painting of a highway rather than at a dynamic, coherent reality. This became a bit frightening because in losing the orientation based on one's usual sense of speed, the placement of oncoming cars, the curvature of the road, etc., one loses the ability to comfortably know what is happening on the road . . . to anticipate variations in the dynamic pattern of what is out there through the windshield.

A disorienting and very noteworthy experience. I was left with the conviction that what we ordinarily do is *construct* the highway pattern, including ourselves who happen to be in it. And this construction is based only partially on what we actually see. It also depends very heavily on the constant, reflexive flow of inferences we make about what we see . . . predictions and expectations built up over years of experience, which allow us to be constantly creating the pattern of dynamic highway perception. Without the constant sweeping of the eyes that is analogous to the sweep of a radar beam, the dynamic pattern breaks down into what it actually is: just objects out there in time and space.

Another point. The daily practice of meditation apparently increases one's capacity to do it in varying circumstances apart from the particular time and place one has set aside for it. One may break away from the narrative, sequential flow of common reality experiences more easily.

Feb. 20
EXTENSION: ENTERING AND LEAVING. The

time seems to require extension; ten minutes is not enough, if only because one puts too much of it into the settling-in process. Today, for example, there was more fidgeting and fussing during the effort to find a good sitting position. This matter of finding the position is itself deserving of serious consideration, for within the general framework of the cross-legged posture, there are endless subtle variations. Any small movement of a hand or arm or foot can change the whole configuration. This is, in itself, instructive, because such changes are often accompanied by a change in the feeling of concentration.

Extending to about fifteen minutes today allowed more scope for exploration of small position changes, the effects of which are significant, but in ways that cannot yet be identified. One is embarked here upon a very great journey and it is much too soon yet to make sure of how it is to be done. Patience. A sense of timelessness. It is increasingly clear that these are the required qualities.

FEB. 21

Suddenly it has turned to harsh weather; cold, grey, very windy, and it seems to be more difficult under these circumstances to enter into meditation even though one is in a reasonably comfortable room, out of the weather. In today's session it began to seem that the meditation effort is rather like entering another domain of the world. To sit quietly in a good position and empty the mind of all its usual narrative ideas, words and images, is to be embarked on a little private island or vessel of one's own. If one thinks of the ordinary stream of life as a river in which we are immersed, then the meditation effort is like climbing out of the river and onto a raft from which, in unusual calm and quietness, one may observe the river in a new way, and, perhaps very important, one may for the little while stop swimming.

The swimming analogy seems very appropriate. Ordinarily we swim in the river of our lives trying to fight across the currents, or, in extreme cases, trying to go against the flow. People in everyday life who appear to be relatively happy, reasonably content if not serene, rather well together with themselves as the vernacular has it: such people are rare. They are going along with the main current of their lives. Stroking to keep themselves above water, as it were, but not fighting against it. But this more or less ordinary state of so-called "good adjustment" should not be confused with the higher state given by meditation. To lift oneself out of the stream of everyday life and float in a vessel of unattached consciousness is altogether different. At the very least, it leaves one with a kind of refreshed, liberated feeling, for the ordinary swimming in the flow of life can be seen as not entirely necessary. Freedom from the oppression of everyday living is there to be had for the taking.

FEB. 23

CONTRADICTIONS.   Much frustration and rapid mind imagery this morning while trying to enter meditation. Counting the breathing repeatedly to get beyond the confusion, which seemed to last a long time. The first five minutes were so bad that for a moment or two I seriously thought to quit for the day. But then everything settled itself very quickly. Quiet and calm came in, and there was a very pleasant, almost happy emptiness, like being asleep while wide awake, and the time sense disappeared. The second five minutes seemed hardly more than thirty seconds. And now, even fifteen minutes after it has ended, I still feel the quiet, warm, contented state of inwardness, and a strong tendency to just smile. What has happened here?

FEB. 24

Very routine today. The problem is always, to one or another degree, turning off mind so that it does not generate ideas and images of the past . . . both real and fanciful . . . or do the same for the future. It seems all too easy to project one's self-consciousness either back or forward in time. The stillness of the sitting apparently facilitates this tendency: no action to preoccupy the mind, hence it runs freer in this projective fashion.

FEB. 25

It seems that a longer time period must be tried. After fifteen minutes today, a very striking pattern began, a fading in and out of the tendency to sleep. It has been typical for some time now that after a few minutes of careful breathing and general stillness, so much relaxation occurs that it feels easy to close the eyes for sleep . . . even in the meditation position. Today, however, when this state developed it seemed that the body could remain relaxed while I brought the mind up from sleepiness to alertness by focusing my eyes a few inches in front of my nose. It was interesting and pleasant to move in and out this way, from lassitude to alertness, and nothing much in the mind except this activity. Another curious item: earlier in today's session it was quite easy to visualize myself in the meditation position in the familiar room, but I could not visualize myself visualizing myself. Why?

FEB. 27

BREAKTHROUGHS. The experience today was more intense by far than ever before. It is even difficult to come out into normal (so-called?) activity to make these notes. Here are the facts. First, there was the usual time settling-in with vague and sharp flows of personal thought. The mind in its familiar playground of past and future, activities done yesterday replaying; activities to be done today, playing in anticipation. Then, better concentration as the breathing steadied down to be unnoticed, the mind became quiet and there was more focus on immediacy. Eyes concentrated on space ahead; window, chair. Some crossing but not a true cross-eyed feeling. In this kind of state after about eight or ten minutes, there came double vision. It was clear that I was seeing out of each eye separately. This went on and became very vivid; two windows instead of one, for example. Then, while gradually raising my eyes higher, there was a powerful feeling of *rising*. Something like goose flesh; a current or a chill, rising from the waist area up along the spine toward the neck. Perhaps it should be better called a strong tingling sensation. It felt very good. As if I were getting lighter. And it felt very interesting, as if it could be played with by moving the eyes down and up, and all the while the eyes were seeing each on their own, more or less vividly, although there were variations in which the two images would move together slowly. All this went on for a substantial time; checking the clock revealed that twenty minutes had passed. My longest period to date. Even now, fifteen minutes later, it still seems good, and one feels still partly immersed in the meditation experience. The outer surface of me is typing and finding the words for description, but an inner core is still enjoying its tingling lightness!

FEB. 29

A very surprising and impressive phenomenon (I could say "breakthrough" because I think it is) today which has so amazed me that I am trying to be extra-cautious in writing about it, lest it seem too pat, too much like one of those "Aha, I've found it" testimonials.

As earlier notes have shown, the meditation is going well. There is the feeling of getting deeper into the mind, and into a changed relationship with body. The double vision and the tingling sensations appear almost as guideposts—signs, so to speak—of penetration. I have not, at the same time, however, given up running, although it is somewhat curtailed as compared to last year.

Today I ran in what has come to be the routine fashion these days; just going easily and with no important resolve to go far or fast. But the running started to go very well after the first mile, in fact, even at the outset it felt much stronger than usual. Nothing remarkable here because one is familiar already with such occasional, apparently spontaneous moments.

At about halfway through the second good mile, however, it came with no particular forethought that I should try to go into the kind of meditative state typical now when sitting cross-legged. That is, simply see if the mind could be put into that sitting meditative configuration. And it worked! There was no double vision but there came quite quickly the tingling sensation rising out of the small of the back and traveling up along the spine. At about the same time, the running strides became more powerful; I seemed to be going along much more easily and lightly. Then I realized that my posture had changed toward the straight spine, upright position one tries for in meditation; that my head was back much further than usual in running so that my eyes focused on distant objects and were hardly able to scan the ground immediately underfoot. And as all this was realized the running simply continued to flow along in the powerful way; breathing a perfect harmony with leg movements, and not the slightest pain or discomfort anywhere in the whole system. Moreover, it felt as if the body were simply going on its own volition in a better way than ever, and as I wondered at this it came to me that I, me, mind, or whatever, was observing all this with delighted detachment. This thing was happening and I was just along for the ride, enjoying it happening, feeling totally one with it, a part of it, and yet quite clearly and profoundly detached from it.

I went for almost another mile in this way, hardly ever scanning the rough ground underfoot, but just directing myself to make a sweep scan of the terrain every five or ten seconds.

After the run, I went into the usual meditation preparation routine, but this time removed clothing which usually prevents getting into the half lotus. I now got into it rather easily;

maintained it better than ever before, and did fifteen minutes exploring very comfortably the double vision which followed the initial breathing exercise, enjoyed the tingling, and felt a new kind of power or confidence in the meditation and the position itself. Everything felt more comfortable, familiar and secure than ever before, including even the muscles that usually balk or only hold their station with effort against pain.

This whole experience is surely a major milestone. I don't expect it to continue to occur at this high level, but suddenly I know much better now what I am doing, and things should go forward in a much easier way from now on . . . at least until I come to the next plateau after this one. It feels very, very good because one senses a command over self and oneness with self as hardly ever before!

3 DISMANTLING REALITIES

MAR. 4

SITTING DEEPER. The duration of the periods is increasing, as if there were an internal kind of force operating to draw one deeper in, or is it further out? It is becoming clearer now that the double vision is merely one sign of how the apparent world outside decomposes when we relax the energies that we usually employ to keep it composed. Just as the visual sense can be allowed to go its own way and produce its own independent images . . . it seems that the auditory sense can do the same. That is, sounds can be decomposed, taken apart from their conventional conceptual meaning and just apprehended as sounds; near and far, loud and soft, intermingling and one at a time. Hence the generalization: meditation seems more and more now to be a means of dismantling, decomposing, taking apart the conventional structure of the world.

As one gets familiar with this process and comfortable with it, the initial dramatic learnings, such as my double vision, become routine and one is led further. One wants to know what follows, what is underneath the surface gloss that one has penetrated. So far, I only feel two kinds of phenomena . . . a great comfortable quietness, and, when this occurs or shortly afterward, a feeling that for want of better words can be called projection. One feels the capacity to project into other people and other places. The thought of another person can occur suddenly in a new way. As if, with self brought to a deep stillness, the image or thought of another can burgeon forth in great eidetic detail such that one feels to be there with them and even more, an inside part of them. Perhaps another way to put it is that being off and away from the ordinary dimensions of living in the world, one understands with much greater clarity the way in which others may be living in accord with these ordinary dimensions.

There came today too, as these notions gain credence in the midst of experiencing them, the thought that it must be such states of being in deeper meditation that lead toward the idea of "astral journeys" or projections through time and space. It is surprising and a little frightening. The conventional world one lives in is threatened in the sense that it seems to matter less than before.

MAR. 6
FEELINGS APART.   Great feeling throughout mind and body of slowness and quietness today after twenty-five minutes. During the meditation itself, there was only much nothing or emptiness. I had thought that as the period could be extended there might come to fill it all sorts of images and thoughts of people and places. But today it was just a good blankness. Good in the sense of not painful, nor particularly dull, and therefore not hard, not requiring much effort. One opens up dead space, empty space. The mind apparently abhors a vacuum, and so to open up some empty space this way is no small achievement.

A few games with the double vision. I could close one eye and get the single image at will; sometimes the two images are so vivid and clear that it seems it might be hard to get back to the single image. A little frightening: one could be stranded with two of everything. Like Noah.

Toward the end today sounds became especially bright in their impact. I seemed to twang with a rush of feeling at any small variation or sharp intruding sound: a pigeon starting its gobbling outside, a distant bell, a spontaneous contraction from the coffee-pot. They sent waves along the lower spine and in the shoulder blades.

With the end of the allotted time, I moved slowly out of position as one learns to do after being still a long time; quick movements seem harsh and hurting. But there was also a very strong sense of still being in it. I watched my hands put my shoes on my feet and it seemed a wonderfully interesting, rich and complex activity. None of it seemed a part of me in the usual way; it was the feeling of quiet and slowness and detachment; perfectly satisfying, perfectly gentle. Nothing going on in the head. Like a double image: there is body and there is mind, and they are separate but coordinated and in harmony. One may observe both.

Mar. 8
TRYING TOO HARD. Very poor effort. Full of confusion and doubt. Thinking too much of sitting positions; mine is very far from the correct postures described in books. This is a problem that gets taken care of somehow when one works with a master and sits under the direction of an advanced practitioner. There is also the subject: a master will provide a focus for concentration by giving a koan, and thoughts of "What is my koan?" kept entering today. One advance, however. The double vision no longer seems to be of any value and I am no longer exploring it. It came today with full conviction; not to bother playing any more with double sight.

Mar. 10

THE APPARENT IN THE REAL: A MOTORCYCLE MEDITATION

Quite fully detached,
The cycle rider going down the interstate at 60

Looks at his shadow on the pavement, and wonders at the koan;
  "Are the lines of the road moving through the shadow,
  Or is the shadow moving through the lines of the road?"

Mar. 11

SIMPLICITIES.   Everything seems to come along as one needs it to come along. The sense of otherness . . . the great emptiness or void . . . absolute Mind as compared to mind in everyday role activity . . . all this is becoming stronger in moments away from the formal effort at meditation. It is very helpful, too. Two days ago, having to travel about a hundred fifty miles by motorcycle when it was quite cold (the low forties) I found myself enduring the cold with much less difficulty than in the past. Moreover, it was possible to meditate. To pull the small mind loose from the fears and discomfort and simply let things be, experiencing the "suchness" of things. Watching distant objects come closer, watching the shadow moving beside me on the pavement, watching even my body as it reacted to the cold by trembling. When it got very bad I stopped. It seemed very simple.

In fact, almost everything seems to grow simple and direct. There is much less to get excited about in general. The motorcycle, for example, which used to be for me a thing of serious excitement and fear is now more and more just another one of the ten thousand things in the world. People as well. The operative phrase of Buddhists is "sentient beings" for people. That's all. Not to be bothered, not to worry. Watch them, watch yourself, be mindful of Mind and mind. Immerse in any particular mind activity as it is necessary but know that one is immersing downward from Mind.

There is nothing dramatic happening during meditation lately. I no longer play with double vision; what is gaining force, however, is the regular sense of the power of meditation that is felt on coming out of it. That is, after fifteen or more minutes of working to maintain the concentration required to slow or stop ordinary mind rambles, then, whatever the result has been, the period following seems different. The return to not concentrating in this way is not immediate. It is gradual, with many brief spontaneous moments of return to the empty mind state one had been concentrating upon.

As for the doing of the meditation itself, I found a book yesterday that contains a fine discussion of various meditation practices, including very useful specifics about breathing. The general purpose and focus of meditation is repeated in different ways but is basically always the same: to know better one's own true nature. *Kensho,* the Japanese zen masters call it.

Mar. 13
METHODS WITHOUT A MASTER.   How to find
the practice that is correct without a master for guidance? Not a bad koan. As the practice grows stronger, both in meditation efforts that are stretching out now to longer sittings (thirty minutes today), and in other moments throughout the ordinary day, there is coming a much stronger sense of absolute Mind. Today, for example, there were longer periods within the meditation that went well as emptiness, or absence of small mind. The experience obtained in this fashion is relative blankness, but not simple dullness. It is freedom from being ordinary self. Why is it so satisfying?

Perhaps the satisfaction relates to the sense of getting outside the cage of ordinary life; the cage we are constantly creating and renewing with our internal dialogues and role-imposed narratives. Words. Ideas of cause and effect, past and future. When all of this is shut off there is openness, freedom, and a luxurious sense of having everything in the present.

To know this is to know that practice is possible without a master. Or, one may practice alone until a master is discovered. Moreover, the many books of the masters are helpful. Reading them tunes the awareness and the sensibility to the great middle way. They offer a form of inspiration and a model. Not the immediate, concrete model of an active, present master, but at least a heuristic general model providing approximate direction. This is quite enough for me now.

Mar. 16
Twenty minutes of very fine sitting today, perhaps the best so far. It was in the half lotus, which I have been practicing now for short

intervals, about five to ten minutes, first thing every morning, sitting on a thin cushion covering the hard floor of a wood and cement basement bathroom. What one sees doing that is the wood walls, the hard tile flooring and the pipes and white sink; a bit depressing and absurd-feeling at first, but getting better and better. As the work on the sitting position itself advances, the hardships of the work, including the things to see, all seem more meaningful, more worthwhile.

Last night there was also opportunity for some sitting, then the hard floor again first thing this morning, and now completion of the "regular" period that was ritualized at the very beginning. What happened in this regular period was only that the half lotus came more easily, and the pain of the position, particularly the numbness in the feet, was quite bearable for a longer time than in the past.

The pain is instructive. One learns more about the meaning of the position itself. Early on, it seemed that it was functional because it kept the feet warm. An understandable virtue considering outdoor conditions or drafty meditation halls. But it seems clear today that the position is also important because of the discipline and mind control required to maintain it against the pain. One learns, of course, that the pain is transitory and meaningless, for in the five minutes or so following the sitting the pain is completely gone. If anything, the feet and legs feel nicely stimulated afterward. So the pain is only a thing of the mind, a kind of illusion teaching about mind. Fifteen minutes ago as I came out of the position the pain seemed very strong and it was hard to get up. Now it is completely gone. Where? If it can go so quickly, what reality can it have? And why then should one be concerned at all with this pain, or with any other kind, since it is solely a thing of mind that can be mastered?

It is like the pain of being very cold or cramped on the motorcycle, and like all of the ten thousand pains that drive us ordinarily through the meaningless circular routines of everyday living . . . transitory stuff of the mind.

Thus, it seems, the pain teaches as one manages it during the exploration of stillness and empty-mindedness. That stillness and emptiness is very busy with the pain, the sounds, the breathing and the sights, let alone the vagrant shifting thoughts of intrusion. So much work to do in the sitting that one hardly has time to notice the pain as anything except one more thing.

Mar. 17

A perfectly clear, sunlit spring morning; only enough wind to know wind exists. A perfect run. Perfect sweating, breathing.

True nature . . . knowing one's true nature, is to know one's fit into the perfections of nature. The universe. The perfection of Buddha nature can be seen in the excellent pine tree which is complete in itself. Complete, unthinking, fitting in; so perfect that all is of a piece: the other pines with this pine, the terrain, the sky. This is what one seeks as one's own true nature. Our Buddha nature is this perfect fittingness. I have had it occasionally in running, very rarely and briefly in meditation so far, and now I know this new thing about it: Buddha nature is just being there and feeling it to be perfect harmony, no need to do, or to think, just to be. But being as a human, not a tree, because we are humans not trees.

Mar. 18

SPACESHIP ME. The meditation definitely grows more natural, more satisfying. Twenty-five minutes today in the half lotus and there was much less pain than ever before. It gets easier, requires less conscious effort to maintain a good position, and there is much more going on inside the mind.

In some ways the analogy to running seems compelling. It is beginning to feel the way running felt as one began to go beyond the first mile. Sitting in the half lotus is less painful, but the awareness of the legs is strong. Today for a bit they just seemed to be *humming* with power and I thought of the motorcycle: it is like being mounted on a vehicle of humming power.

And then there came as has come before an awareness of great busy activity. There is so much going on! The breathing; the direct visual and auditory inputs (just by turning the eyes slightly one sees whole new pictures of what is immediately out there); the images of people and places that well up out of the mind. In this connection, while doing the work of meditation, trying to observe the mind process and find its origins, there seems little doubt that subtle, apparently spontaneous thoughts get triggered by sense inputs, and these thoughts are quickly enlarged upon by the mechanism of association. Then, as they enlarge into a sequence (usually involving cause and effect "if one were to do this, then such and such would follow") one becomes easily absorbed in the narrative, and, consequently, once again sucked into the workings of small mind. So to be aware of this, and to be familiar with the process, is something of an advance, giving one a new sense of knowing what is happening, and how it happens.

Perhaps the total busyness of meditation can be put in the metaphor of spaceship earth. Only in this sense, as one conducts the meditation one seems to be conducting a flight of the spaceship ME, mind and body. There are all the activities of the spaceship to be monitored as one glides along in its flight: small power and trim adjustments (breathing and the legs) to stay in the proper configuration of half lotus; internal events in the control center of small mind; and then the observations to be made and the inquiries to be pursued when all the maintenance is in order. Given all of this activity, twenty-five minutes begins to be a short period. Within the flight period, however, there is also beginning to show up very brief moments of powerful transcendence. Moments wherein one feels perfectly free, untied from the spaceship and all its doings. These moments are what it's all about, seems like, and it seems further to be no accident that they come along simultaneously with the sense of being just perfectly configured in the position. The zen master Roshi Suzuki has said that satori is a perfect position of sitting, and whether or not this be true, I can see where it comes from . . . albeit only briefly.

Mar. 19
UNITIES. Twenty minutes on a warm, breezy, sunny day. About the weather; noting it seems a fair idea because it is very much a part of the ambience of meditation, although I don't know yet how to describe its significance. It just feels significant.

In the early morning, first thing on arising, the discipline of sitting is going very well. Even though it is a relatively short interval of about fifteen minutes, it is a good way to begin the day, and it seems to make the subsequent, longer period better, perhaps by "tuning" one's being in some fashion. There is certainly a sense of facilitation gained from the early period.

A curious puzzle has begun to show itself today. The very quiet sitting, as noted earlier I think, tends to set the mind free. One feels and experiences the conventional mind quite apart from the body. If anything, there is an almost palpable feeling of detachment from the body. Yet the masters usually speak of gaining unity and a conviction of oneness from meditation. Why then does this divided, separated experience occur? The problem rather quickly shaped itself for me as a sort of koan. In a book of koans studied recently I discovered a long list of sayings that are employed in koan work, and one of them came back to mind as being close to my "mind-body" separation question: "The willows are green, the sky is blue." This is a statement of figure and ground in the Western perception tradition. Hence (maybe!), mind and body only separate as figure and ground depending upon one's perspective?

4 TECHNICALITIES

MAR. 22

LESS FOOD, MORE STRENGTH. A new thing learned: fasting. It is extraordinary how, once a serious beginning has been made on the path toward knowledge of one's own being, unexpected new discoveries turn up. Having experienced this a few times already, it doesn't surprise me that it happens, but each time it does, it seems a great mystery.

Meditation has been going well, but other practical activities imposed by the necessities of family life have been contributing familiar corruptions: moments of frustration, boredom, anger; the many little disgusts that seem so typical of ordinary living in middle-class American society. Of course, people deal with these things. There is whiskey or pot; there are the movies, the TV, sports, hobbies, etc., but such diversions are, ultimately, hardly anything more than the equivalent of repeating nonsense syllables or saying prayers. One has to *do* something. And the doing cannot be a running away because there is no place to run. Going inside through meditation is clearly of immense value. To do this for moments outside the regular meditation periods is excellent, but difficult. The analogy that has occurred to me is that of parachuting out of an airplane. ("OK, folks, I've had enough of this dumb trip for a while, I'm getting off; fly it yourself!")

Going without food released a strong form of energy this weekend that allowed me to walk through an upsetting situation. Had to attend a competition for youngsters in another city, taking mine along for their turn. Very atrocious. Middle America at her worst. How to ward it off? How to keep equanimity? How to avoid projecting personal feelings that would disturb the children's pleasure in this thing that had come to mean a great deal to them?

The way that came to me was utterly simple. In order not to take it out on them, I could take it out on myself. That is, give myself something important to do, a task, equal to theirs. Next to breathing, the most simple thing we do is eat. Not to eat is to feel hungry; to feel hungry is to have another reminder of mindfulness, of the need to maintain awareness of self, of mind, of what one is doing and not doing in the immediate moments of living. So it seemed like a fine idea to live on only liquids as much as possible during this interlude of immersion in a social hardship, and it worked beautifully.

The only way to describe it is as a feeling of power or energy. As if the fasting generated from within a kind of force field that kept out the emotional poisons which in the past have tended to build up in me on these occasions. One simply felt stronger; it was possible to go along with the flow of the routines of driving and chattering and arrangements-making without being contaminated.

Somehow, and I don't understand how, the going without food seemed to link together the meditation periods with the other activities of the situation and the effect was to smooth them out. It may not sound like much, but to take food only once in twenty-four hours provides a deeper sense of meaning for those hours. It is a way of bailing out that doesn't require jumping. One can be in the scene, as it were, but at the same time be aware of having something and doing something that is secret from the others present and yet allows connection with them without being trapped or contaminated by their problems. Maybe it is pure power. Power over oneself in this most fundamental of ways being somehow equivalent to gaining power over one's situation.

MAR. 23
COMMENTARY. Roshi Suzuki said that in meditation one may simply let the thoughts of small mind flow as they will, it is only necessary to watch them in stillness making no great thing, no great discrimination about this. Merely sit in good posture and let mind flow on until it empties itself.

Garma C. C. Chang, another master of the older Chinese School, said to cut off all thought in meditation. The "work" is to stop the flow of small mind thoughts. His advice is to put the mind in a condition as if it had just been shocked, and to cut off all thought ruthlessly, the moment it appears.

KOAN: WHICH IS THE WAY TO WISDOM?

Sometimes the wind blows in fierce gusts.
Sometimes the air is perfectly still.
The moon has many phases,
And sometimes in running and sitting
There is pain in the legs.

MAR. 24
WAYS TO SIT. It's becoming a stronger and stronger conviction now that this activity is going to be a very, very long-term affair. Just sitting, like running, is turning out to contain within it a whole world of variations that get more and more interesting as one becomes more and more aware of them. There is, for example, what might be called the technology of sitting. One may purchase special mats or cushions, or both; the cushion to be used under the behind, the mat to be used as a resting place for the legs. In this connection, it seems now that my earlier sense of needing a master who could at least indicate correct sitting positions, was false. It is much better to find these things out alone, discovering for oneself

which posture seems to be best. One comes to know this by an awareness of solidity and strength and generalized confident security that emerges rather immediately and forcefully and spontaneously as one gets into the "right" position. One knows it is right because it feels unmistakably right; the feeling fits the model that has been described in the writings of the masters.

Consider, furthermore, all the variations within the generally "right" position: tensions and pressures that can vary through a great range as the legs are tucked more or less tightly into the half lotus. There is a growing awareness of an optimum leg tension that produces almost a literal *humming* sensation around the knees and thighs. One feels mounted on a powerful vehicle. But there are also all the other variations, ranging from very small eye movements to perceptible turning or raising or lowering of the head. Then there is the placement of the arms. In some traditions of meditation they say to extend the arms so that the wrists or heels of the hands are way out there on the knees. (And it seems a long way out there, because one picks up the picture of the hands in the lower left and right corners of the visual field when practicing in this position.)

Meditation is, therefore, a practice with infinite physical ramifications and variatons, which take quite some time to explore. Just the physical practice of meditation, in other words, is quite enough to keep one occupied. So I am beginning to think how foolish it is to be in a rush to find great things happening in the mind, when even the small physical aspects noted above, and including the many variations of breathing not noted, are in themselves complex enough to require much exploratory effort.

Mar. 25
SURPRISE. Positioning of the body is improving at a notice-able rate. It feels to me that so far as sitting in the half lotus is concerned, a real breakthrough has occurred. I feel more and more comfortable with it now. Maybe comfort is not a correct word. Better to say simply that I feel *with* it; it is no longer alien or strange. All progress in these matters is always surprising. After you learn to just do the practice as best you can, whatever it is, and then find that no progress occurs no matter how you try, and then you go on doing it anyway, out of stubbornness, faith, or whatever, and

then you find yourself no longer even thinking anymore of progress, then, somehow or other and in an unexpected way, something happens and you suddenly know you have made progress. Really know it. This process has occurred in a few large ways and many small ways during running and already in the meditation, yet it never fails to amaze me. Of course, others also report this; it is a thing that apparently helps to bind serious students together.

MAR. 26
BLANK SPOT.   Very odd and a little disturbing; no proper meditative state could be achieved today. Nothing, that is, comparable to the deep quiet dropping into the emptiness that has come to be so familiar. What is curious is that there doesn't seem to be any reason for failure; no unusual events, no sensations following from dramatic happenings. The only outstanding change is the weather, which has turned very gusty and grey: tornado weather in the Great Plains. Could this disturbance be a kind of premonition? If the area were hit by a tornado this afternoon it would indeed qualify me as a sensitive mystic, but it's all very dubious. More likely, some hidden springs of my concentration have slipped away, momentarily, from the discipline. Perhaps I have come to take the discipline too much for granted and slacked off without any conscious awareness of doing so?

MAR. 27
MEETING A PILGRIM.   Nothing happened, but the sitting this morning was much better than yesterday, although not even close to the more powerful experiences of a few days ago. Perhaps we have in us interior oceans that ebb and flow like tides. In a given period of days, the tide may rise to a startling degree, but then it cannot be held or trapped into remaining at its high point. Instead, like water (the great instructive metaphor of Taoism) the inner oceanic tide of one's being recedes to its ordinary level. From this standpoint, the failure yesterday can be seen as only a conspicuous recession; a falling back to ordinary mind, even though this ordinary mind is becoming less ordinary. One gains

mastery over it and clarity about it, and if the high-water points cannot be maintained, one knows they exist and this very knowing changes things.

Knowing has many odd ramifications. Example: A few days ago an old friend of several years who has been on a path he calls mystical visited for several hours. I know his mysticism is serious, and I respect it, while also knowing that his way is very different from mine. But we talked of our different ways; the experiences that are either analogous or shared in common, the books studied, and the practices followed. Rather like two parachutists, or priests, or auto racers comparing notes. Later, the next day, reflecting on the visit, it suddenly seemed to fit many of the things I have read about Buddhist monks and masters in Tibet and China. They would travel a lot, and when meeting another like themselves they would immediately fall to discussing their work along their paths, always speaking of the central experiences of meditation in much the same way as my friend and I. Those who know, share, and attempt to clarify their knowledge to each other. It seems universal, a manifestation of the One Mind.

Mar. 29

Some small, further adjustments in my sitting posture support pad (adding a large plastic bag filled with folded paper sacks) has seemingly provided just the additional "lift" needed for a very full, solid, and happy half lotus. There is great satisfaction in finding a good position that can give such strong, valid feelings. It is like hitting a perfect tennis stroke, or making a perfectly controlled sequence of turns on skis. To know the perfect position is to know what it means when the masters say: "Yes! That's it!" Hitting the target is what it's all about, and to pursue the sitting with this purpose is possibly a good beginning toward pursuing one's life in all its manifestations with this purpose. To try to hit the target, the "sweet spot" as they say in golf, in all the doings of one's life; this is one way to express the essence of Buddhist practice.

There is always more to do, however. To gain a very good half lotus is to wonder at the thought of what a full lotus must be like. In Jewish tradition, there is a ritual toast which says: "Next year in Jerusalem." What we need here now is an equivalent for sitting:

"Next year (or someday) a full lotus." Meanwhile, not to be greedy. The sitting just completed was no small blessing after the sloppiness of the past few days.

Mar. 31

Excellent position, excellent stillness, excellent focus on being. The sitting went very well and the calm sense of penetration toward the deeper, true nature of one's being is retained now well past the period of the sitting. I am beginning for the past few days to try to do a little brief reading just prior to the meditation; something from the Tao, or from a talk by a master welcoming students to a meditation period. The words sink in the mind not as ordinary words which conjure up thoughts and concepts and images, but rather as signs and signals pointing to silence and stillness, and to the dropping of concepts and images. Taken in conjunction with the practice itself, the words seem to help me go deeper into mind, that is, true mind rather than ego mind. At the same time, however, there is a hightened awareness of body: tingling skin and the low, humming vibration of the legs. A peculiar contradiction, this matter of deep penetration mixed with greater awareness of the surface, but a contradiction that seems less and less puzzling or unnatural. It could easily be true that what we have learned to perceive as a contradiction is in fact no contradiction at all, but rather a false learning.

5 LARGER VIEWS

THE VIEWER AND THE VIEWED.   The sitting in
meditation is one of those things that begin as a great hardship and
test of discipline; matures after a time into something of a luxury
(it's so wonderful to *have* this thing, etc.), and then seems neither
hardship nor luxury but rather necessity, like eating and sleeping.
Why? Maybe it is like getting used to wearing glasses . . . or better,
perhaps, like having a window into mind, a kind of personal TV
screen showing always the same feature: This is your life.

Centering on one's being, considering the pattern of one's life
(Karma?), immersing in the thought-flow that surges and ebbs
around the stillness and dark quiet of the core of being, one feels
over and over like an actor watching himself on the screen. The
thoughts projecting outward are invariably of self. Ordinary self,
roleplaying selfish self. One tries to pursue them backward from
the screen to the projector: where are they coming from? Follow the
beam of light down from the images on the screen to their source.

That's the strategy. Yet it fails. All of the pursuit action and backtracking only leads to emptiness. The projector turns out to be nothing . . . a vacuum. Yet there is something. One knows it even though it is not visible.

Today there came a few moments here and there of double vision again, and it occurred to me suddenly as this happened that that's partly what this business is all about! Ordinarily, we see only one visual image with our eyes, despite the fact that there are two out there, superimposed on one another. This is what happens when one views he small mind thoughts and images. There you are on the screen, but it's only one of you, the public, culturally programmed and determined you. Underneath that is the other, core you. True self. And through the practice of meditation one begins to be able to see that there are two. The viewed and the viewer, as it were. With more practice it gets easier to separate them.

Most striking here is the associated sense of disgust that wells up in relation to what one views. That is, the viewer . . . core self or being . . . is more and more disgusted with the public roleplaying cavorting dummy out there who seems to operate so frequently like a puppet, responding to all the cultural-social conformity strings that are attached to him. One way or another, those strings have to be untied. And if the puppet then collapses in a heap, too bad for him . . . hard cheese. The whole puppet show will close and if the dummy star is stranded in Philadelphia we won't even send him carfare.

APR. 5
MACHINERY OF LITTLE MIND.   Time statements seem to have dropped out of these notes lately. The sittings have been averaging about twenty to twenty-five minutes. Today was twenty. Time is not very important, however, and by unwittingly forgetting to record the time one sees just how insignificant it is. When the sitting practice began, even a few minutes seemed a terrible long time; now it seems nothing. This may follow from the steady discovery of all the things that need doing and attending to during the sitting. So many things to be done that it almost seems appropriate to go into the sitting with a kind of strategy mapped out: What points of interest shall be observed? Which gateways

will one take? Is the focus to be inner or outer? Endless decisions, and all of them totally meaningless, of course, because one doesn't decide anything. Instead, it just happens.

Today it happened via the outside gateway of sounds. It is a warm and sunny-clear morning of perfect spring weather. No wind to speak of, and the sounds of birds are quite prominent. Listening to them it is easy to recognize the workings of little mind, because the tendency is to focus not on the sounds themselves, nor on the silences between them, but rather on one's anticipations of repetitions. Each little input is enough to set the mind to anticipate the next. Following the moment of sound there comes an almost immediate small tension of expectation for the next moment. If the sound does not come, the tension quickly mounts. There is a kind of thirst to hear that next sound; mind has, so to speak, predicted and promised the repetition and if it does not come something must be wrong. And mind therefore proceeds to work on this something that must be wrong. To have a small prediction of little mind disconfirmed is, after all, a threat to the whole machinery, and so more and more of the machinery comes into action. What a fascinating nonsense it is. This is the way we build the false world of our illusions. First, by making our predictions, even these very little ones, and then by justifying them, by rationalizing the outer world to fit the preconceptions we have of it. If the bird call does not continue there must be a reason, or even several reasons. Mind goes clipping along in this fashion, preventing understanding or perception of that other world of silence and spontaneity, to which forecasting the future is completely irrelevant.

Apr. 6
THE ENTREPRENEURIAL SPIRIT.   The routine of practice is mantaining itself according to what has become a familiar pattern: five minutes in the early morning, close upon wakening, then twenty or so minutes, later in the morning, after taking care of household chores, other maintenance activities, and just prior to beginning the work of the day.

Three noteworthy events occurred today. First, just prior to the twenty-minute sitting, a passing glance at the picture of a sitting zen master must have impressed me more than I was aware, because during the first several minutes of my own sitting there came a very powerful sense of dissatisfaction with my position. It is simply nowhere near to being the proper way indicated by the picture. Mind machinery began to run with this dissatisfaction. How to correct it? It would be possible, and quite practical, to consult a local yoga master who gives instruction. And if he is too busy probably one of his advanced students would be willing to give instructions or coaching in how to achieve a more proper half lotus (heaven knows I despair of the full). Minutes went by in circular speculation and rational planning about this matter. But the real questions then emerged. What is it I want here? To look like a master? To achieve a more graceful pose? To impress others with my accomplishment?

If, indeed, my half lotus is awkward, is it not a matter that may better be approached via my own concentration rather than the technical aid that could be given by an expert? The thing is to be worked on alone, perhaps, as part of the practice. And then too, there is the possibility that the unsatisfactory position is in itself a reminder, an instruction, something that imposes humility. It hardly seems possible for a person sitting awkwardly to become arrogant about their practice!

So the wheel turns. I recall feeling quite set-up and happy about the sitting position a while back, and now that very same position seems poor. Some kind of American escalation here? Does it come from living too long in a culture of planned obsolescence? Is a better position desired in the same way as we have learned to desire better cars every so often?

All of these thought-runs were shut off, finally. Focus shifted inward. Concentration was upon an object containing lovely swirls of wood grain. There represented in the object was mountain terrain and ocean waves. Everything is in everything; one is impressed with this more and more.

Final event after completing the sitting: a strong conviction that it may be time to start planning a visit to a zen center later this year.

APR. 7
INSIDE QUIET.   This twenty minutes was very quiet, very still. Small mind relegated very much to the periphery of things

while the center sense of self, just plain empty self, seemed much stronger today than it has been before. Position seemed more satisfactory; steadier, although it is not seriously changed from yesterday. The breathing went very nicely; calm and smooth and reduced. There was very little movement within the sitting position as compared with other occasions, and the time went by more quickly than usual. At the end, and now too, a few minutes after the end, I feel very calm, peaceful, and with mind at rest. No great joy of any sort, but no worry, no tension; just a quiet, solid-being feeling. It's very good.

Ordinary programmed living is rather like a merry-go-round. The sitting practice takes one off the merry-go-round. One steps away and looks at it. The result is calm detachment, a view of the spectacle of one's ordinary activity as if seen through the eyes of a moderately interested third party.

APR. 8

Nothing this time like the quiet satisfaction of yesterday. Instead, the feeling now is of exuberant energy! An exclamation point; that's what it feels like now, whereas yesterday it felt like those signs for pauses (. . .). How strange. The practice is the same on both days, yet the result following one of them is an empty feeling of satisfying pause, and the result following the other is high energy: smoke slowly curling versus bright flame. What mystery in our human condition!

In today's practice there appeared for the first time an awareness of change in my visual focus upon objects out there. Earlier on, the main focal point had been a bright semicircle of glass placed on a window sill about five feet away. But for the past few days the focus has been shifting to a dark spot on the grainy oak leg of a work table about three feet away. The objects are very different, and it might be significant that after all the practice to this point, one begins to find satisfactory focus in a much less dramatic object. The thought is that this may mean that one is quieting down, needing less from the outside.

There also came another koan: why do all the masters invariably direct attention to breathing? I have had various answers for this in the past, but now, today, while concentrating on breathing, a new answer arrived. We must scrutinize our breathing

because it is the primary essence of life. Nothing is more fundamental. Everything begins and ends with breathing.

APR. 10–12

ONCE

Once I rode a motorcycle through rainstorms two days for 750
miles . . . to see a woman who now thinks differently.

Once I gave up a good part of living for three years to write a
great scholarly book . . . which now sells for the paper, by the
pound.

Once I thought I had killed a guy in a fight that started over a
woman . . . she later went into psychotherapy to get me out of
her head.

Once with shaking knees I spoke to 3,000 people to discourage
them from doing mass violence . . . which they wouldn't have
done anyway.

Once I became the father of a baby whose total life span was
three minutes . . . now I have two children who will probably
see me dead.

Once I went regularly to sleep on images of violence and my
own heroism . . . now I count breathing and wonder at how
mind fills the emptiness.

Once I thought the world could be stopped by going very
fast . . . then I thought the world could be stopped by
being very still. Now I have no preferences.

APR. 13
FIGURE AND GROUND.   If there is any singular thing
that meditation insures, guarantees, it is that one will become
aware of the chaotic, self-serving, and illusory nature of mind.
Lately, this awareness has been extending outward more and more
frequently, spilling over beyond the sitting periods and into the rest

of the day. As this happens the sitting itself seems less important or noteworthy; just another thing among the ten thousand things one does, no better or worse, distinguished or undistinguished, than brushing the teeth or tying the shoes. Why bother with it then? The most immediate answer is that it helps—just like brushing the teeth and tying the shoes. Another answer is that it carries one along a path leading out of the garbage heaps of ordinary mind. What seems to be happening now is that as I get a bit further along this path, the perspective on the garbage opens up. There is almost a literal perception of some distance now between me and my garbage, and I find myself looking at it with new eyes of wonder, surprise, in many different situations other than just the sitting. The sitting, therefore, is becoming more of a background than a foreground activity. It is important not for itself or in itself, but for what is following from it.

APR. 20
LOSSES.   A great gap of time since the last notes. It seems much longer than a week. I am also, quite literally, "out of practice." Four days spent on a vacation with family with no serious sitting practice has set it back considerably. This morning, twelve minutes seemed very long; the position was inadequate; it was necessary to fight off the fidgets; and, worst of all it seems, mind kept running along stupid repetitive tracks concerning some awkward business business-professional matters. The lay-off time has definitely been very bad, and I understand at least one thing from it: why the masters go into retreats every so often. It must be out of a sense of disgust at the failure of true mind to sustain itself strongly when practice routines are upset by mundane activities.

APR. 21
SLOWNESS.   Sitting quietly in the practice is slowing down everything; this is the experience that was missed during the past few days of no-practice. One cannot perceive the flow of the stream, and gain self-awareness of one's place in it unless one is relatively still. Otherwise, one is flowing with the stream and cannot perceive the movement. It's very elementary.

The practice today was much better than yesterday. Less interference from conventional mind doings. The satisfaction, and the calm feeling of self-possession, has come back stronger today. Yet from having had the break I can see how fragile is the path toward enlightenment. Trying to live one's being in accord with the understandings of one's Buddha nature is so difficult because activity is in itself usually inimical to deeper realization of one's condition. The thing is to find a level of harmony between activity and no-activity, so that, as the zen masters say, one may do everything and do nothing.

APR. 22
TIME-ENOUGH TIME.   Meditation *time*—twenty minutes today—is becoming a more and more meaningless idea. Just another empty concept. Today there were moments of good concentration and clear awareness, and there were moments of discomfort and struggle to maintain a reasonably correct posture. So the general timing seems foolish because the quality of the moments is what counts, not the total number of minutes spent making the effort toward proper quality.

Immersing into one's breathing, attaining the best stillness possible, one begins to perceive the ceaseless activity of the world of things and people, including the part one plays in it. What this does is provide a sense of separation and release. Becoming aware of the bonds holding the self to the larger, encompassing structure of things and people allows perspective on that structure. Perhaps what can happen is escape. Like the astronauts, one might build up sufficient force to reach "escape velocity," and thus get out into pure space, the full freedom of universal mind. But the simple practice of daily sitting is in itself a great satisfaction. To reach that deep, pure space of absolute mind is probably going to be impossible. In fact, it hardly concerns me anymore because it is enough to have this other sense of having grasped the possibility. Deep space is ideal; to have got one foot barely an inch off the ground is immediate and real, and it is enough.

APR. 23
A NUGGET.   A brief but extremely satisfying period today. It was calm, good positioned, and filled with quiet pleasure following

from a sense of powerful command. It felt as if universal mind, or higher self, or whatever, had just come in and assumed control. The ordinary "I" (body and sense of self) seemed to be inhabited by a superior being . . . like being taken over by a visitor from another planet. For a moment it occurred to me that there seems to be a wise old monk in control here . . . just watching ordinary me, slightly amused and immensely tolerant.

APR. 24

DIALOGUE. After about ten or twelve minutes of good sitting, that old zen monk who has been living very quietly and cleverly inside of me now for . . . who knows how long . . . a year or so maybe, well, he came out in plain sight today, for the first time, laughing like hell at the antics of this clown of an egotist . . . this monumental professor who thinks he has got hold of some wisdom because he can count the breathing pretty good and even remember occasionally to push the diaphragm low, and clear the decks by saying Mu! to himself.

That old monk with the face of Roshi Suzuki roars with humor, slaps his thigh, pointing at the fool with his aching knees and careful pretensions at not moving the head, who thinks he is working on zazen! And in between laugh gusts the monk says: "What the hell do you think to get from this? You violate every precept of true knowledge every day . . . do we have to list all of it, from intemperance to judging good and bad?" Yes indeed! One cannot help but join in the fun. It's true. There I sit, trying, by sitting, to maybe remove one small spoonful of the everyday garbage, and yet in the rest of the everyday activity I am piling in garbage by the shovelful. This is the situation, in fact: one small frail creature working delicately and hesitantly with a spoon, against a huge brute of a stoker who shovels in huge globs of junk .whistling country-western tunes all the while to cheer himself through the silly rhythms of garbage collection.

What a realization! And yet it leaves me delightfully happy! The laughter of that old monk is so contagious, and so utterly true, that one cannot help but laugh with him.

6 ΠΟΤΗΙΠG ΤΟ ShOUΤ ABOUΤ

MAY 1

INTERRUPTION. A few days, break again, this time for purposes of attending a professional conference. There were two days with little meditation worthy of the name. There was an early morning run through pleasant country terrain, and then some moments here and there during the working conference when I was able to go very nicely into a proper state of meditative awareness, a kind of "Mu" state. During an after dinner speech of terrible nonsense, for example, it was possible to focus on a candle that made wonderfully symmetric patterns of shadow and light. Sleeping in a strange place, I also found that each night a good sense of stability and proper awareness could be gained by counting breathing while lying in the dark. On the fourth and final night away, after missing plane connections, it was necessary to sleep in an airport motel, and here it was possible to switch off the TV about ten o'clock and maintain a proper, good "sit" for a half hour. One useful result of all this is a new appreciation for the use of "Mu." It serves very well as what the masters call a skillful means, whereby one may snap the mind, just by saying an inward "Mu," into an awareness of the larger context of things.

It is noteworthy that the confusion of travel by plane and professional activity in a strange context was ameliorated by Buddhist awareness, although there was much strain as compared to ordinary routine. This is signified by the sheer relaxed and renewing pleasure one feels on returning to the familiar pattern of sitting, eating, sleeping, running, and reading.

No special sense of discovery or enlightenment follows from any of this. Instead, there is only a feeling that the effort to practice zen is further confirmed. It *does* make a difference; even the small degree of practice I have achieved is significant. During the conference, for instance, which included scholars from Europe as well as America altogether numbering almost 150, it became quite obvious that with only one or two exceptions, there was absolutely no feeling from either the words or the actions of any of these people that they had any sense of Buddha mind, Buddha being. What prevailed throughout was the egocentrism of academics. It was, indeed, a very solid, palpable atmosphere of narrow egoism. Small, self-centered ego minds working at their very best to impress others with their erudition and concerns for the state of the world. Invariably narrow, frequently dull, and occasionally disgusting.

I could detach, stay out of it, but I could not do anything more. Perhaps some day something more will be possible.

May 4
DAILINESS.   Shorter periods for the last two days. Ten minutes at twilight . . . the first time for me at this part of the day . . . was extremely satisfying yesterday. And the same brief period this morning was also very good. More significant, perhaps, the sense of mind awareness is with me quite often during other parts of the day, and this awareness provides a sort of instrument that may be employed to protect oneself against many of the stupidities of everyday ego activities. Ego is a manager or impresario of the self: it tries to put the self into the best possible

situations; to make the self at least a star, if not a superstar. In this way, authentic living, genuine awareness of reality, is always being destroyed or corrupted before it can take proper root.

May 5
NO DRAMATICS.

Nothing much happens anymore, it seems. Sitting in meditation for twenty minutes this morning brought only the quiet, simple things already noted many times in the past: breathing, sense of body position, familiar watching of small mind tricks, shifting the focus of attention from vision to hearing, and so on. Yet there is much quiet satisfaction in the activity. One feels it to be a proper tuning up of the total being, and in addition, a practice that somehow makes other things different. This cloudy, rainy day for example, I found myself noticing with full attention the reflections and ripples in the occasional puddles of water. How remarkable those puddles are when they are seen not through the mind of concepts, which immediately relegates them to the category of trivia—dirty rain puddles—but rather through the cleansed vision indicated by the term "suchness." That is, as things in themselves, rain puddles give quite fascinating sensory experiences: colors, forms, dynamics of movement and the like.

So what? So, this is one place that the sitting effort produces. A place of mindfulness that can offer some wonder and pleasure even as one walks along the familiar way to work in the morning, among people who are all apparently so locked into their "going to work in the morning" resolve that they seem to see nothing at all. (And of course, having done it myself for so long, I know what not seeing is all about.)

Where I am now is at the point of no dramatics. Along with brushing the teeth, eating, and sleeping, sitting in zen meditation is a practice of everyday life discipline followed because of its manifestly beneficial effects.

May 6
MU!

I think that what is happening is that simplicity and watchful non-doing is becoming more a part of me, and this explains why there seem to be so few dramatics lately. If true, this is a major event!

May 7
NOTHING IS SOMETHING.

There seems to be nothing worth saying that hasn't already been said in these notes. Yet, as all of the large things have already been said and experienced, it seems that the experience of meditation begins to involve small things. Today, sitting in good position (one knows good position very simply, because it *feels* like good position) there came a perception of rhythmic, vibrating resonance, as if my whole body were moving ever so slightly back and forth, as to a metronome . . . The sensation has occurred before, but this time I attended to it, whereas in the past I have been too busy with other things such as breathing, listening, and seeing. And it slowly began to appear quite clearly that this subtle resonance could be felt only when one had achieved a solid position of perfect stillness.

A contradiction? In such stillness one detects resonating movement? The answer is, of course, yes. For there is no absolute stillness in life. There cannot be. What was going on was my heartbeat. Never before detected or experienced with this degree of clarity, the very essence of one's being alive is finally known through this means of quiet sitting. The resonating rhythm-beat of the blood as it is continually pumped through the body. It sets up a counterpoint to the more obvious and much slower rhythm of breathing. Like a two-piece band playing on and on! Mind flow and imagery? The doings of ordinary mind? These are overlays on the basic two-piece pattern; they put the melody line upon the basic rhythm. And like all melody lines, they are the more obvious and more demanding elements in the ensemble. In fact, most of the time all we are aware of is the melody line. Our perception tracks along with the melodies and hardly ever acknowledges the underlying foundation provided by the rhythm section.

It is all quite striking in a way, this steady pattern of moving down through the layers of one's awareness, penetrating through one level after another of melodrama, each of which seems as nothing once it has been passed.

MAY 11

ITNESS.   It's quite unmistakable now; things are changing. The sitting is feeling less and less important, but at the same time more and more satisfying; the experiences of daily life seem less and less mundane, and more and more mysterious . . . arbitrary and surprising. One walks among them out there, most of them, as a visitor from another planet occasionally. Most striking of all, little experiences are growing more important. It was surprising to feel a great sensory joy just on leaving work yesterday and getting into the superb spring day. Somehow . . . it is happening . . . I see more in the sky, trees, soil and pavement . . . and feel it making me *smile* with something. Not exactly happiness, or wonder, or joy, although it seems that way at times, but rather because there is just a smiling, shake-the-head *impressiveness* at the feelings that come now . . . at the *it*ness of things, and the *it*ness of me-*with* the things.

MAY 12

SOFT MANURE.   A soft, gray-green morning of gentle, almost imperceptible rain. A day like this is a gift from heaven, and I take it as such; savoring the walk of about a mile to work, enjoying the grass and trees, making a good tea when arriving at my place, reading a bit of Roshi Suzuki on the posture and breathing of zazen, and then getting arranged nicely in the position to immerse into mind on this floor that has become such a familiar friend to the body that sits upon it.

Twenty minutes, more or less, some segments with eyes closed, even though this is against all the teachings. How can one explore the teachings properly if one never deviates from them? Moreover, my eyes need the rest, and after one brief period of having them closed, and hovering on the edge of sleep while keeping good position, the eyes open up and the visual scene seems suddenly very brilliant, bright and colorful. A fresh vision of my place and myself.

Nothing to shout about, of course. Mind still ebbs and flows with moments of emptiness succeeded by moments of indulgent imaginings, but this stuff no longer seems important. Trungpa, the Colorado Tibetan Lama and master of meditation, says that we should use the imaginings and garbage of the mind as a good farmer uses manure: to nurture growth. There is no feeling of confidence that my mind-manure is yet nurturing anything in particular . . . only the feeling that the manure is somewhat less oppressive and dictatorial as compared with the way it was earlier on. This may or may not be progress, but I like it, and it's enough. One could live on a hell of a lot less.

MAY 16
DIRECTIONS.   Yesterday, I planted a young avocado plant. The day before I rode a motorcycle for hours through a hard rain. Today I sat in good meditation. Tomorrow, I will be on a high mountain in spring snow. What does it mean? Wouldn't we all like to know!

The more the doing of action, the more the realization of non-action. Sitting is intensely instructive of this point. One sits and one marinates in the doings of the mind, and all of it . . . especially the watching of mind doings . . . reveals and exposes how little difference any of it makes. Even the sitting makes no difference except that it is good to know what can be known in this way. One penetrates closer to the center of things.

Above all now, there is a great sense of being in passage, of hanging in between two points or stations. I know something of where I began, and that is already rather far away; quite out of sight. I know little or nothing of where I am going, but there is emerging a sense of it somehow. In the beginning there was hardly any direction to be followed except not following any special direction. Now, there is a sense of being in the right direction . . . that this direction will lead on toward a large and full place . . . a promised land of one's being. In fact, one knows already something about this because there are so many other things that were formerly significant that are now not only insignificant, but actually just empty and dead. I am going toward a warm glow on the horizon . . . that's the direction, and it's all I need.

MAY 22
MOUNTAIN ACTION.   Much activity. Climbing on skis and on foot at higher altitude (about 11,500) than I have ever been

before, it seemed very clear how the Tibetan mystics would have come to their extraordinary mind-body feats, as well as their ordinary harmonies. At such altitudes, all the conditions of existence combine to impose instruction. The limits of the body and the powers of mind stand out in relief, as it were, because of the hard quality of the environment. One can only act in a deliberative fashion . . . partly because any sequence of overly-quick movements brings intense pounding in the chest (breathing is of course a major conscious process) and there is always the necessity to place the feet correctly while moving on icy snow crust or jumbled rock and gravel. There are few if any flat places permitting conventional, automatic, walking. One is forced to a rather narrow focus on the immediate situation because there is so much that requires attention. In this sense, to merely be in the very high mountains is to be in a meditative framework, for immediacy is everything.

May 25
KNOWING THE WAY.   There are no benefits; there are just "no preferences." In the cool, sunny morning today I ran about four miles, and now have done about twenty-five minutes of sitting. Both activities were smooth; no notable disturbances of mind or body, no sense of disharmony, discord or struggle, but no particular feeling of happiness, or pleasure either.

It begins to seem, therefore, that the ego-less no-preference state of being is beginning to emerge. The practices one has learned no longer seem either amazing or amusing. There are no great dramatics because all of the qualities of experience during these practices have become familiar. Yet they are not routine, and if there are no great dramatics on the one hand, on the other it must be said that there is no boredom, no monotony, no feeling of sterile oppression that so often accompanies behavior practices that are routinely a part of the active, real-world mode of life.

The running brought what the running always brings: rhythms of body interpenetrating mind, the zen-dialectic experience of my early entry upon this path. The sitting, in turn, brought what the sitting has been bringing now for some time: awareness of immediate realities, observation of mind-workings, garbage and no-garbage, fullness and emptiness. None of it matters in any sense that can be put into words. One becomes more and more like a tree or a mountain. One is just "there" and the words are superfluous; trees and mountains do not express themselves with words.

Is it good? Yes, very good. Why is it good? I don't know. Part of the conviction that it is good comes from the feeling of having got a long way toward the real core of things in one's existence. It is knowing that the earliest principle of Buddhism and zen that first cut into the mind is true. When the masters say that zen is ". . . to eat when hungry, sleep when tired," I know now in a way that I didn't know before, how utterly perfect and profoundly correct is the saying. Another part of the good is this strong feeling of kinship with the masters. When they say the Buddha is in everyone and everything, I feel their truth confirmed without words, because lately in the sitting practice there is the feeling of connection with the masters of the past. One feels their discipline, their humor and their power to transcend power. Thus, having heard recently of the so-called supernatural powers of a sufi from India, the natural reaction is laughter at the foolishness that people demand of their gurus, but also an understanding that the guru probably offers little miracles in order to make the path more accessible to the small minds of the seekers who follow him. Wisdom of the masters comes in this way . . . without knowing by conventional evidence, but knowing just the same. It is very good. It is another signpost on the path to the core.

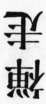

7 IN NO-MAN'S LAND

MAY 29
PLATEAU. When these notes were begun, they seemed to be important because there was nothing like them; no record of experience concerning day-to-day meditation effort was available. The records of spiritual activities that were available all seemed to deal with the "higher" things and give little or nothing on the very concrete level of what happens in just sitting.

It now appears to me that the reason why so little practical material exists is that those who make genuine progress in meditation come to see its true emptiness. The emptiness is very important, of course, and it is duly noted, but there is not much that can be said about it.

Today, for example, the good half hour of sitting just finished seems nothing, no more or less important or noteworthy than the activities done before or the activities to follow. Yet there was this period of time immersed in the usual observations of thought, the

counting of breathing, the attempts to maintain proper positioning and receptivity to the sounds and sights as well as the inner
mental flux of ideas and imaginings.

What does this mean? Perhaps nothing at all! Or better yet, it
may mean whatever one wishes it to mean. It is quite possible, of
course, that one may after a time simply reduce meditation to just
another routine activity like eating, breathing or defecating, and
in doing so destroy its mystery and its value as an intimate
instruction of one's human condition. From this standpoint, it
could be maintained that ego has again pushed itself outward into
a new territory, leveled the terrain, and gone about its business of
constructing just another mind-suburb, a development with the
usual split-level structures of conventional thought.

More likely, however, it is something else, because it feels very
strongly like something else, and relevant evidence from other
aspects of everyday life also suggests something else, which is: that
a plateau has been attained. A no-man's land. No longer is the true
mind bound and blinded by everyday ego or self, but not yet is true
mind fully free of its bonds and blindness.

Deeper cutting through to the core is required; the hand that
holds the cutting edge is ready and knows its direction, but the
flesh beneath the edge trembles, and the hand remains poised,
unwilling or unable to go on with it in the face of fear; or maybe
just indifferent for the moment, knowing that the flesh will steady
itself in time and thus call out for the next cut.

May 30
TUNING THE INSTRUMENT.

A good and simple
effort. After a long run through a grey, muggy morning, the
sweating is intense and it seems to make a very nice foundation for
going into the sitting . . . not directly, of course . . . it takes time to
peel off the clothes, mop with the towel and putter about with
sundry little things as one slows the body activity.

Sometimes while running, I think (visualize) sitting; sometimes while sitting I think of running. But then, in both these
activities it is clear that one may think of anything, including the
activity itself or its very opposite. Mind is indiscriminate and quite
voracious in these matters.

The pattern in the meditation itself is regularizing into an ebb and flow: sitting in position and counting breathing initially provides a fair start. Then as the breathing is slowed and the body is steady, the eyes fixed on a familiar point and the senses all quite open, mind will start its usual flow. Even as it starts, one knows it, and there is not a temptation to cut it off immediately, just as there used to be temptations to nurture and cultivate the flow of ego imaginings. But lately I am trying to follow the teachings of a master who suggests that in meditation we should neither resist mind flow too much, **nor** yield and go with it too much. I like this. The master speaks of meditation in analogy to the way a musician speaks of tuning a violin: strings must not be too tight and not too loose.

Nowadays, the flow of imagining seems to be ending more quickly than it used to, and with less effort. As this happens, one slips into the no-thought state, aware of breathing, aware of sights and sounds, until the flow of mind starts itself up again with material that cannot be easily silenced. And the ebb is succeeded by flow again.

One thing new to be noted. While sitting, there was a sudden noise outside, to my left side. It was a moment when the position was very strong, and the state of meditative concentration was quite deep, and what happened was that I did not move or even blink or catch breath, but the whole left side of my body responded by seeming to go suddenly chilled or numb. There was an intense tingling all along the left side, somewhat like the feeling one gets anticipating that a bucket of cold water were going to be thrown onto the naked body. Perhaps this is an example of how the body may respond to an event on its own, prior to the mind. This is probably something fairly important.

June 3
FLOWER GURU.   Today turned into a commemoration of Buddha's flower sermon. Some time ago I had placed a geranium plant on the sill of a small window that faces me during meditation, and the window itself has often been a focal point for concentration. This morning, after being away for a day, on

settling into a good position I saw a red flower: the plant had put out a bloom, and it seemed extraordinarily rich and stimulating against the usual background of sky. It brought immediate pleasure and an "Ah, good" sense of satisfaction. One would not say, of course, that the flower had bloomed at just the right time to aid the meditator, and that this was just another example of metaphysics in action. Yet the mystery of so-called coincidence is increasingly suspect even among highly reputed Western scientists, so perhaps there is something else here after all, or else something that needs to be created.

In any case, the reddish-fuschia flower just stays there now. And having immersed in it during the sitting, it seems even after the sitting that it has a special, personal quality. It remains in place in its perfect flowerness, and we, the flower and I, have a relationship; the flower instructs me on the nature of being. Being what it is when it is, and non-being as well, because it will be dead soon according to the way people reckon time, but it shows not the slightest concern. Nor do I.

June 5
STEPPING ASIDE.   During the sitting this morning, after settling in with good breathing, there came the thought, "What is meditation good for?" The answer, of course, is that it is good for nothing and good for everything. In the past several weeks I have drawn upon the experience of meditation . . . the attitude or orientation inherent to this activity . . . in many different situations of hardship, both physical and mental. One finds it coming to the surface of mind, so to speak, quite regularly and spontaneously during moments of tension, moments of fear, and moments of irritation or anxiety. And what it does is make calm where there has been turbulence, smoothness where there has been roughness. It provides detachment from ego, a sense of there being something other than the self; there is just one's total being and it is so foolish to get disturbed over the ego or self part of one's being. Better to simply stand aside from it . . . don't struggle with the wretched beast, only see it as another construction produced by mind to fill the emptiness.

JUNE 12
SEEING CLEARLY.   It is getting harder to make notes on the meditation efforts. The rigidly determined attitude toward this recording effort is just now what it was at the beginning. Now, it seems mildly foolish to think that there is any serious point in making notes on the sitting. It won't help me in any important way, and it can hardly help anyone else. Besides this, a more important consideration is that there is so little to say. One sits, one tries for a good posture (but not to excess), and one experiences the workings of mind in all its outlandish nonsense, and one tries to attain stillness in mind as well as body.

All the "rules" or guidelines for meditation seen in the writings of different masters seem to be shaking down quite as they suggest. It has come to be easily understood, for example, that to try very hard is wrong, and to not try at all is wrong. One literally comes to know this, and all the relevant aphorisms of zen and Chan Buddhism, such as "There is not two; there is not one either," all seem much more sensible and clear than they used to seem. So what is the current status of realization? Well, to begin with, there is no single way, there are many, but they are sort of all the same underneath their apparent differences.

Then too, there is no "right" and "wrong" if one is seeing clearly. Thus, it might seem that to let one's mind wander long enmeshed in garbage illusions and imaginings during the sitting is wrong; but seeing it clearly one may simply know that perhaps the mind requires more of this sort of thing occasionally, and the mind-doing may be instructive. The same with posture: all the masters generally say that it is good to try for the classical cross-legged posture, but that in and of itself the posture is nothing, or rather, just another one of the ten thousand things. To see clearly is to know that compulsion in either of these instances does not necessarily guarantee anything at all, and may even be just another form of immersing into egoism; another way of trying to *prove* something. The spiritual materialism discussed by the Tibetan master.

On the other hand, to see clearly is to gain more and more a sense of doing just what one properly requires in one's being, and to be confident that one's being knows this. So it doesn't matter if one sits for ten minutes or thirty, or if one misses a day or two entirely, because in *this* business, in this journey on the path toward freedom, there are no scorecards and there are no milestones. So how does one know where one is? Well, it's not easy, and it's certainly not verbal. It's rather like the knowing one has in the process of making a clean shot in tennis. One knows.

JUNE 15
COMING THROUGH.   There has been some good further grasp of the situation in the past few days; a new and certain understanding about this routine stage of meditation. It is, very clearly, the consequence of having practiced sitting to the extent that it is no longer an ego-dominated affair. It is no longer the heroic, unusual, or dramatic thing that it seemed at first, when it was a hard thing to do. The ego, striving always after heroics and unusual, special qualities, has been brought to a standstill now so far as the meditation is concerned. And this seems to make it just another thing . . . routine, too dull or boring to write about, because there is no more novelty in it . . . no more ego-trip heroics, in fact. And this means that it can now be pursued, practiced, in a new way, the way without ego, where there are no quantities to count, and no visions or illusions to recount for myself or some possible reader.

What all this means, what has clicked together in these past few days after reading some Buddhist texts and teachings which happen to concern the states of being ego-full or ego-less, is that yet a further sense of knowing the correctness of the path, so to speak, has set in. Consequently, the meditation is done much more freely and directly than before. The time of day for it has shifted, partly because of a changed summer schedule of work. There is freedom, too, in the knowledge (that has just seemed to emerge with full conviction) that one needn't be so much concerned with posture, duration of the sitting period, or levels and varieties of "interference thoughts" during sitting. It's just all there. What? The surge of confidence in the way of meditation, and the sense of doing it in other forms all through various moments and activities of the day. One has it while walking to and from places, while out on the tennis courts, while running for the exercise and liberation of body, while picking peas and lettuce in the garden, and then cleaning them in the kitchen. *It* is coming through.

June 21
BREATHING.   It came as a thought, rather suddenly and while doing something or other unrelated to meditation (if anything is unrelated, after all), that when we breathe we literally and concretely *do* become an immediate part of our situation. We literally mingle together with physical reality by pulling in the air, transforming it in our body . . . and having our body transformed by it, of course . . . and then expelling the air in its new form. Back and forth, in and out, moment after moment, this tangible transformation of ourselves by the environment, and of the environment by ourselves, is going on and on, and usually without even the slightest awareness.

Moreover, in this way we literally intermingle with the being of others . . . those who share the air with us. To be in a room is to be in a relationship with whoever else is present; sharing the same air . . . their influence upon it effecting our experience of it, and vice versa. Here is a terribly concrete specification of what it may mean when people speak of sensing the vibrations of others and reacting to them.

The air is the first medium for life, for communication. This seems to be the genuine basis for concern with breathing in Buddhism: the recognition that in taking air and expelling it, we are bound to our immediate situation in the most basic of ways. The latrine and the locker room; these will instruct on the meaning of breathing!

June 24
FLOATING.   Unexpected tasks, minor emergencies of every-day life, have prevented both sitting and running for the past few days, but it seems nothing because one has the expanding sense of all things just happening as they should in any case. Moreover, the meditative state can be approximated under all sorts of circumstances besides private sitting. One simply dips oneself down into it: driving a car some distance, sitting in a committee meeting, on awakening and on going to sleep.

A lovely little variation came the other day while out with the children. They had along a kite, but went off to do something else. It was a perfectly blue-sky, moderate-breeze situation. I flew it up, then lay back on the grass and simply immersed into the kite against the sky, feeling the breeze, listening to the sounds of children in the distance, and being up there, out along the string into the air. Sensual, delightful moments of no-mind doing! They have always been lovely, but the meditation practice has given them, endowed them, with new depth. One knows much better how to do such things properly. . . . One knows to switch off the car radio and drive along immersing in the experience of time and space.

The sitting practice may do nothing except sharpen the sensory awareness of things. If so, it is enough. To experience the immediate reality of present moments, one needs the ability to feel, see, hear, just what is going on in the present moments. And to have this ability, one must master the mind-narrator that is always moving or manipulating the awareness either into the mind-created future or the mind re-created past. Or, and this is what happens when listening to the car radio, one may place one's mind into another mind and feed from its creations: we hum along in the song created by another, or exchange our own internal narrative for the narrative being offered by the newscaster, commentator or story-teller.

Lately, it grows easier and easier to see and know these things. At the same time, it is clearer that one grows more aware of immediate things. Sounds, for example, are more and more felt through the whole body; breathing grows ever more salient in many different ways, and vision . . . vision is so enhanced that it sometimes seems as if one has just landed on a strange, rich, new planet full of amazing sights.

Another new practice should be mentioned. For the past week or two following each sitting period I have been resting; lying down, allowing the eyes to close and then just drifting with the restful state . . . sometimes to sleep but most often into that twilight area between sleep and wakefulness. It's a splendid, luxurious feeling. No focus, no concentration, just floating.

JUNE 28
ALTERED STATES. Perceptions, sensory processes, are changing now during the sitting. The shifts to odd eye crossings, or

muscle movements influencing visual perception, occur more rapidly and more freely than they used to. The sitting itself is done with less in the way of dramatically salient discipline; less self-conscious effort to adhere to the "rules" or the ideals of meditation. One just sits in the flow for a time.

Resting afterward, eyes closed, or slightly open . . . in that in-between sleep and waking state . . . just *feels* very correct. It might be that it is conducting toward even a truer form of meditation than the cross-legged half lotus position.

Mind immersions; going down in the submarine . . . ruling out or keeping out, with little self-imposed effort, all thought of the things one *ought* to be catching up on . . . all thought of the guilt and anxiety feelings that work is primary. Being what one is, is one's work. Nothing more, nothing less.

June 30
TENSIONS OUT.   Today's sitting and the resting that followed it were both marked by a very noticeable feeling of vibration in the body. That is, feelings of temperature changes in the hands and torso, and sensations of movement in the surrounding environment. All of this seems to be an outflow of tensions, as if the sitting in really good meditation sets the body free to be itself and to do its things more spontaneously than it could otherwise. First the senses . . . vision and hearing, and now it seems more and more the skin itself. Hands folded together in the mudra clasp, today seemed to be ebbing and flowing with tension very spontaneously, and with no variation of any sort being deliberately imposed. In fact, there was this sense of ebb and flow in synchrony with breathing in and out. Quite rhythmic. And all of this completely without any sort of deliberation or predisposition set up by any reading or other form of preparation. New experiences just seem to emerge like this, and my conviction is that they are entirely legitimate. I *know* that the sitting today was very good, and very deep. How does one know? Because there is no phoniness, no falseness, no seeking after something with intention prior to the event.

July 8
THOUGHTS.   Several days since the last notes were made. Much activity, and some interference with the sitting routines, but

one comes back to it as to an old friend these days. "Penetrating thought traps"; that's what it's about. As the meditative efforts carry into other aspects of living, it becomes ever more clear how the perspective gained through sitting allows a different practice of life. So many situations are so much easier to deal with. Even the situation of not being able to sit in the accustomed routine of meditation is not a problem. Or, it is better to say, it is a *thought,* and a thought only. If one wants to make a thought a problem, of course, one can do so. Most things one calls problems are really thoughts. For example, having missed meditating for a couple of days one may grow upset and frustrated and say "I'm missing it, I'm screwing up, I won't make it, I'll lose my progress, etc." Sheer, arbitrary, nonsense. By what standard except thoughts is one to judge the proper time interval for meditation? Time is elastic; it lies in the mind. A friend says he is sorry to be going away for a month. He would not say this for a day or three or four days. The idea of the full month seems a lot; it may be a lot, or it may be nothing, depending on what happens. Just as a day may be a lot or nothing depending on what happens. Here one enters into the meaning quality of time, as a runner enters and engages the meaning quality of distance . . . sometimes a mile or two is a great deal; sometimes it's nothing at all. It is all in thoughts.

July 12
MONOTONY OF MIND. One observes the routine qualities of the fantasies and imaginative contents of mind when allowing it to run freely off the leash. There are repetitive patterns that become very dull from sheer repetition . . . always variations on the same few themes: work, sex, and vague detached events . . . like fragments of films put together haphazardly. It becomes a bore. Perhaps this is one of the things one is supposed to learn after a while . . . that the doings of mind let loose from its anchoring points as ordinarily programmed by social situations, are really rather a bore in the end.

   In fact, this is why we turn, most of us, in one way or another, to prefabricated versions of life in films, TV and the like.

8 THE GATELESS GATE OPENS

JULY 26
RUNNING AGAIN. It seems a long time between notes. The recording of meditation had, indeed, more or less ended because there was literally nothing more to say, certainly nothing more was "happening" than what had already happened and been noted. The only change I was aware of was in regard to the growing familiarity of the meditative state, which of course means all of the various kinds of mind-body experiences (a whole world of them) that can go on while just sitting.

So now what? Comes again, as it has come already maybe a dozen or more times before, one of those "happenings," a new thing, very, very heavy indeed, and one wasn't at all looking for it. The old unexpected zen thing: by giving up, one succeeds; by letting go, one captures; by surrendering, one is victorious. Unbelievable, but again true, just in this past three to four days.

It is the running. When I began the meditation effort I

thought the running had given all it had to give . . . there would be no more qualitatively new knowledge to come from it. So the effort became sitting. Not that running was simply forgotten or given up entirely. It continued, but less so than before, and with no particular sense of spiritual focus or concentration. I had more or less given it up, and certainly considered that it had been, so to speak, "used up."

Now, for the past few days, I have found myself running well as *never before,* double the distances, and it is as if a new world has opened! In the past, the running was in the two-to-four-mile range. Now, in just the past four days, I have three times been in the five-to-seven-mile zone. Today, after about two and a half miles this morning, the crud of very conventional academic work seemed to mount up and I was suddenly feeling a tingling physical desire to go again; either that or have a large hero sandwich and a large beer. Kill the tingling sense of unused energy . . . or pent-up tension . . . swamp it with food, or let it burn away by a long run in 90-odd degrees of heat. It was the latter. And the result was incredible . . . a literal sense of mind and body operating in harmony and watched over by the third force one labels as spirit. In the shower after doing five miles there came an amazingly powerful, detached feeling of quiet joy in just being; just tasting a few mouthfuls of water as it flowed from the shower head. Just walking became a quiet delight. Everything seemed different, more potent: the body itself, the surroundings, the sense of movement and of taste.

Why is the distance run such an unbelievable experience afterward? I don't know but I have a guess. The running itself was not terribly painful or hard. Yet during the last mile there was a sense of having to be very careful . . . one thinks of the stories of people who have dropped dead of heart failures this way . . . one notes the feelings and looks for signs . . . any pains on the left side? (a few years ago I had them), any sudden, pointed aches in the chest cavity? How is the breathing? In brief, there is much monitoring during the last mile, and there is a great sense of being a rather fragile, perishable item. Some slight dizziness came and I slowed the pace for it.

The extraordinary feeling of knowing or seeing "suchness" after the run may come from the fact that during the last stages one feels close to the edge of death. Any mistake or serious false move, and the body which has been slowly stretched to its capacity in the first three or four miles could snap . . . something may break inside and that will be it . . . either death or long disability. Yet the run continues, the fear is managed as one might manage it balanced on a ledge high up above some rocks. One runs through it very carefully. The body becomes a six-foot carton of eggs . . . not to be jarred or dropped. Playing with it, however, one has a sense of playing with death, because this *feels* like the zone where people die very easily.

The ability to make this new penetration must come from meditation. Couldn't ever do it before. But now, having "given up" on running, it seems to be possible. No clearer zen lesson was ever given.

JULY 29
SOME HEAT.   Over five miles in very hot temperature today, but much easier and less impressive than on earlier occasions. The reason? One adapts; one learns the tricks and tactics of self-preservation in the new environment . . . the five-mile-plus zone . . . and one gets very smart very quick. In this instance, I varied arm movements and gaits much more than before, to prevent the numbness from setting in, and it worked. It also made the activity seem much less impressive afterward, because the impact was reduced by new tactics . . . Marvelous, however. One runs in a meditation, or at least part of the time with an image of meditation juxtaposed to the image of the running. Everything going nicely down the track together in 97 degrees of heat.

JULY 31
PATTERNS.   Twenty minutes of what I now think of as a proper, formal meditation as compared to the varieties that occur in other ways through other activities. Going back to the practice of sitting and mind watching in the more formal way brought back my old self-given koan of earlier sittings: "What is the pattern of my life?" Today, the correct answer, the zen answer, came almost immediately and with that full conviction one comes to recognize

as the guarantor of correctness in all things Buddhist: "There is no pattern to my life." There is only being, suchness. Any so-called pattern is merely the imposition of an artificially created (culturally dictated or programmed) framework, which appears to reveal cause-effect pathways, sequences, continuities and consistencies . . . the things we are taught to think of as patterns. There are no patterns except for the ones we create, or those others create and then put upon us, or offer to us so that we may put them upon ourselves. It is for this reason that anything is possible . . . and, anything may also be impossible. Possibility is only an inference. Some inferences seem better than others . . . more accurate, predictive, but none are perfect, and all are, therefore, illusions.

The problem for most people, of course (and me too, until this recent small advance of understanding the reality of "no understanding"), is that once a plausible pattern seems to be "theirs," they tend to make it true. Accepting it, they wittingly or unwittingly force themselves to follow it. And then everything gets fixed, sterile, dull, and oppressive. Once freed from the belief in patterns, then every event, even the very small ones like eating, sleeping and breathing . . . let alone seeing and touching and creating . . . is quite literally a new adventure! A unique new happening never exactly like anything that occurred in the past, and never to be exactly duplicated in the future. This is the wonder and joy the masters have discussed as the experience of "suchness."

The longer distance running of the past weeks has opened up new realities to me very directly. Breathing is an M-G-M Technicolor extravaganza with a cast of thousands (of cells, of course!). In this new experience of time and space relations, one becomes a nuclear physicist of the mind and body by getting down to the small particles. Life and death seem so much closer together and one works and plays with them carefully, yet wonderingly and joyfully. It is maybe like this: as a soldier, I remember, the truest freedom from oppression of the military could only be achieved in a no-man's land, a zone of hardship and danger such that no conventional authority would go out there with you, and if they did, there was no way they could order you around. So it is with the ordinary mind, the "officer commanding," when one is out in the no-man's land beyond five miles. There is no choice here but to hope for grace . . . for harmony, and to allow the body its full scope of intelligent liberty. Working in the five-mile zone is like opening the mind cage and throwing away the key.

The odd thing about all this experience is that it has only formed itself to be put into these words, after again sitting with full commitment. So I see it as a pattern, perhaps, that is no pattern. By releasing my purposes in running in order to do sitting, I have made immense advances in running. And by releasing the purposes of sitting in order to do running, I have made advances in sitting. The quality of clear contact with truth or reality that has just come out of today's sitting is manifest evidence.

Aug. 2
A SMALL MIRACLE.   Call it a miracle . . . say that anything is possible . . . a little over seven miles round the track today . . . 28 laps. And with perfect ease! After starting out a little slower than usual, thinking only to make the by-now conventional five miles, it seemed that the deeper I went into the run, the better and stronger it felt. At mile four, where the action has usually come down to hard resolve and concentration, and where in the past one has felt just a bit on the edge of fainting here and there, today it felt very strong; stronger than at mile two. Consequently, I just decided to go on with it, through mile five. At six, there was no great difference from five, and it went right on to a strong finish at seven.

Quite a miraculous feeling. Like another world out there, and it takes a while to come back into the ordinary one. Why did it go so well today? The weather is one factor. Instead of the 90 or 95 degrees it has been for the past few weeks, this afternoon it was only about 80. Breathing was noticeably easier today too. Maybe this has to do with the coolness. Even after finishing, the walk to the shower was noticeably easier than it has been in the past after five miles.

No explanation can completely demystify this thing for me, however. There are no strains, no feelings of cramp or stiffness or aches in the aftermath, just as there were no panting gasps or painful steps during the run itself. The whole thing has been strictly a perfect zen experience! The arrow has, indeed, shot itself this time. A meditation in action.

Aug. 11
A LARGER MIRACLE. It should be noted for the record
that a few days ago, pushed on, I think, by the same kind of
emerging conviction that will lead a monk to roll his sleeping mat
and set out wandering in search of new teachings, I made a
completely new run, and could not complete it, but ended worn
down to nothing; rubber-legged, drained of body fluid, and almost
unable to walk back to the start point.

The impetus to this run came while circling the quarter mile
track round and round one hot day, making about seven miles. It
seemed then that if one were to go out cross-country, the variability
and novelty of being on entirely new ground could well make the
running easier. Variability of terrain might reduce the tendency
toward stiffening up. Novelty and challenge of new scenery, new
environment might stimulate mental focus to a higher level. There
was also the image at this time of Olympic marathon running
recently seen on color TV. And above all, a sense that grew
stronger and stronger of the need to journey outward further than
before, to see what instruction might be gained there.

I haven't yet got round to measuring the total mileage
involved in the full circuit of this cross-country run. Rough
estimate is ten to twelve miles; including one very substantial hill
and several smaller grades. The main hill is about at the half-way
point. Until that point, the run went very well, and it seemed
certain that it could be completed. The heat was about 90-odd
degrees when the run began at 2:30 in the afternoon.

The hill reduced me. I got over it by recourse to small steps
and hard, piston-like arm work; then went another mile on dead
flat ground, then coasted a while along a shallow downgrade, but
finally broke after working up and down two smaller grades. The
break came slowly, and was in fact no actual *break* but rather a slow
reduction to final zero . . . inability, except at the price of very
serious pain, to continue even the smallest of running steps.

There was more intense soreness in the arms, shoulders, and
neck than I can ever recall having in the past. Breathing was good,
and heart seemed strong and without great strain, yet there was
also a pain or soreness never felt before in the lower area of the
chest and upper abdomen. Above all, however, the final decision to
stop running came slowly, ultimately enforced by the sheer numb

rubbery quality in the legs. They simply would not go forward on their own anymore. The analogy fitting this situation is of tired, worn-out infantrymen who are ready to surrender. Like regimental officers, elements of the mind debated among themselves: should we go on or surrender? First it was decided to stay on in the action a little longer . . . perhaps the changing ground would allow the troops to recover themselves. They didn't. And the support systems were starting to fade, as noted. Breathing remained strong enough to support regimental headquarters, but even here things were beginning to go slack, a tacky, dullness set in, as the possibility of surrender grew more and more probable.

The decision to stop grew during the last quarter mile from a real possibility to a certainty supported, in the end, by full consensus among all the elements. (The "officers" all knew that no purpose was to be gained by driving the tired troops forward with the flat of their swords.)

And so the stop, the transition from running to walking which, considering the very, very small running pace at the end, might seem to be nothing but instead, as every distance runner knows, is always very painful and hard . . . almost as much but not as much as going on. Because with the added new pain of moving stiffened limbs in a freer way, comes also the knowledge that this pain is on its way down.

At first, the walking steps were easy, but they quickly became hard as new points of soreness emerged to replace or reinforce those that had retreated with the end of the running. My estimate is that at the stopping point there was still another mile and a half or two miles to go. After a while, I settled into a brisk walking pace and it seemed it would be easy. But it got harder. Briskness couldn't be maintained for much more than a half mile. Thigh muscle pains. Toe and foot pains from what seemed to be incipient blisters (none were found later). Continuing pain in lower chest and abdomen, novelty of which raised fears: maybe one had pushed the troops too far?

The walking steps became shorter and shorter, and we all struggled in under that hot steel sun, naked except for short shorts and tigers on the feet. It seemed to take a long time, the last mile, and it did. It was about 5:10 when I reached the shower room.

What did it mean? In the days since, I have not thought of it much. Recuperation was fairly quick. No great muscle cramps; a mile run the next day, and then longer on the days following. One thing is that for the next few days there seemed to be a new, rather independent or detached quality to the legs. I could look at them . . . found myself looking down at them . . . as I walked or ran, noting what seemed to be a new subtle kind of muscle definition in the thighs and near the top of the knees. The legs, in short, appeared to have a more clear-cut life of their own. But this sensation has faded out now. Meditation proceeds as usual. I find myself thinking now of making that same run again, yet knowing that I won't do it for some time. The run is there, waiting quietly, in the way that I suppose mountains wait quietly in the minds of mountain climbers.

Maybe this is the instruction gained. There is a new hard and seemingly insurmountable and relentless presence in the mind now that was never there before. Like finding a new and puzzling, intimidating, yet powerful guru, that the monk knows can offer important wisdom if he, the monk, can prove himself worthy in the eyes of this master. They always say it, the great teachings and stories of Buddhism, that the apprentice must be able to risk everything, and discard anything, in order to progress along the path toward enlightenment.

This sense of having been broken by the run in both body and mind is powerful . . . it draws one back. It requires more perfection of the mind-body harmony. Lately while running, there is a kind of mandala in the mind's eye: a great crane gently waving its wings in the upper left corner; an image of myself in cross-legged meditation in the lower right corner, and in between, larger and in the center, me running.

Perhaps this running is as close as I can come now to the wandering of the mendicant monk. It is a pilgrimage in search of instruction that is in fact, no wandering and no pilgrimage, because it is all right here. Not bad really. One could do much worse.

Aug. 13
CLEAR INSTRUCTION.   Experience strikes again . . . it is such a wonderful teacher, and so beautifully cruel, without the slightest elements of mercy.

After all the advances and progressions of this past few months . . . the meditation work progress which has no measure, and the running progress which has too easy a measure, and can therefore deceive more easily . . . after all that, and the arrogances, egotisms that must have gone along with it . . . well.

This morning, I awoke to great pain in the small of the back! Could hardly turn to see the clock without pain . . . could only get out of bed with the greatest effort and clever tactical planning.

What an instruction; from the challenge of several miles, to the challenge of moving several inches . . . all one, requiring the same discipline, tenacity, and the rest of it. No master, no guru, could program one's path to better effect!

And the cause of it seems instructive too: not the rigors of distance running, but only a rather casual tennis match early the other morning, during which I reached out to stroke in one direction while I was in motion in the opposite direction. A move made thousands of times before, yet this time it brought a moderate twinge to the small of the back, which seemed only a trivial, minor discomfort until this morning. So now, after liniment and heating pad, I can move well enough for routine affairs of the day, but always feeling some pain, and the problem of several miles is now the problem of getting out of and into chairs. Superb. One moment is a thousand years; a thousand years is one moment. How foolish to be concerned one way or the other.

Aug. 14
MORE KNOWLEDGE.   The action is heating up. A very solid twenty-minute sit this morning in a stronger half lotus than in the past. I have tightened it, by clasping hands much more firmly together than in the past; this holds one up much more solidly, and although it creates more muscle tension the position is stronger. Strange that I haven't come to this before . . . maybe the penalty of being without a master to teach it, yet how much zen there is in the fact that one's conviction of correctness is enhanced because the change has come about on its own! And why the change? That damned back problem. It's receding now, but still hurts enough, so that when getting into position this morning (unlike the past few times when I have just been cross-legged not

half lotus on account of the pain) it was necessary to do something different. The sore back has been the instructor here.

And then the real action. In the position, counting breathing in the same way as in running, one naturally thinks of the running. So again came the question, or koan maybe, of what to make of that long run to the breaking point . . . mileage of which I still haven't measured, which could be a good sign of progress toward less ego . . . and the answer came just like a white light bursting in the mind. *One may break oneself in meditation just as one may break oneself in running, and vice versa.* Having read several times of the "heroic" meditation *sesshins,* especially the extreme once a year *rohatsu* when monks meditate about seventeen hours a day or more for seven days in a row, at the end of which they are literally broken, it suddenly connected. The run was a kind of sesshin for me, a very small scale rohatsu.

What the monks gain from their heroics appears to be greater clarity. Stripping away all extraneous mental and physical doings is an aid toward realization of the no-self or self-less self: the mind awareness that is beyond verbal consciousness.

For me, all the practices are connecting together in new ways: the running and the meditating are much more now like the very same thing. Furthermore, certain professional work in hand has required some study of the philosopher Wittgenstein, who finally concluded that language was, in effect, a kind of fraud. "Language bewitches reason," he suggested. A beautiful Buddhist statement, although the zen masters would go further (like the Taoists do) to add that there is something of greater importance beyond both language and reason. Wittgenstein apparently felt this too, and spoke of "the will," of right or "correct feeling." But he seems to have stopped with something like empathy between people as his concrete formulation. Buddhism goes way beyond empathy . . . embraces empathy, yet sees it for what it is as a low-level emotional reflex, and suggests not merely simple empathy with or between some people, but *empathy with the whole universe.*

One can feel as much with a bird, tree, or brick wall as a person one likes or "prefers." This is at least Taoism. In zen, one who knows this and experiences it (how? by being able to see that there is as much worth watching in a plant or a rock garden as one ordinarily might watch in an extravaganza film) can ultimately throw it away and live somehow in the total freedom that comes with total harmony . . . Given a film to watch, the zen master might enjoy watching it; given a brick wall to watch, he enjoys watching it. Sensory experience . . . the perception of color, form and all, is indivisible. When the old masters could sit for hours in front of a wall, it was because they might have been experiencing the movement of a shadow across the wall as being just as fully a dramatic action of universal forces as C. B. DeMille ever created in one of his Bible epics.

What a reality . . . no, what an *awareness!* What a *truth!* One is tempted to call it "satori" . . . how funny that sounds now. Here is the aphorism that came to mind yesterday while examining Wittgenstein: "To know about knowing, is to know there is nothing to know." (I have this powerful feeling of strength, authenticity, correctness. I have eaten no meat for this past week.)

Aug. 15

A point of order. Today I took time out to finally measure the distance of my long run . . . I shall call it the Long Run from now on in imitation of the Red Chinese Long March . . . or maybe it should be called the Rohatsu Run. I hesitated to measure: what difference would it make? If it was shorter than I had thought, I might be very disappointed; longer, and I might be very puffed up. Hence, no gain possible. But since I thought of it at a time when I could do it without much inconvenience, I thought: "Since you finally thought of it when you can do it, you should probably do it." Maybe deeper down there was fear that to measure the distance would be un-zennist . . . but of course, to worry about being un-zen is, clearly, to be un-zen!

The total distance of the thing is 14.8 miles. I broke at 11.5 miles. Now that I have been over the thing again, I know it can eventually be done. The reasoning mind goes to work on it . . . quite automatically . . . planning strategy and tactics. The main hill, for example, starts at just about mile six. Therefore, one needs to save everything until that point, as was not done on the first try. Everything considered, especially the still sore back, I think the next go will not be until at least a month or almost two months from now: mid-fall. Then, perhaps again in mid-winter, on one of those clear cold days with no wind. And again in spring. If I don't make it by the spring try, then I will surely do so next summer.

Knowing what I know now, I know that it is no great thing . . . no great vehicle of enlightenment, only something to do while waiting . . . a way of marking time on the path. But it needs to be done. I want it. The monks in monasteries shovel manure, scrub floors and so on, besides their real work of meditation, and it is helpful. This will be helpful in the same way. It is a chore; menial and low like washing dishes seems to be, but it is also a psycho-physical koan.

9 SUDDEN KNOWLEDGE

AUG. 15

Things are tumbling through my mind like a cascade of water that has been suddenly released . . . sudden knowledge . . . insights . . . realities.

I was just in a bookstore looking for a certain work by Van de Wetering. Before I could barely get past the doorway, I saw things I used to read automatically, upon reflex actions that go all the way back to when I was 10 years old and first discovering that libraries offered not only the greatest escape of all, but one that was more socially approved and more effective than comic books. One was first programmed, and hooked on it when we all read the garbage comics, Batman and all, as kids, identifying and having vicarious thrills. And when, from about age 10 to 14, one worked up to better stuff, like Jules Verne, Rice Burroughs, and the simpler H. G. Wells, it was really all just a matter of becoming a heavier and heavier *entertainment junkie!* Like going from grass to pills.

Further up, like in college or late high school, when reading more and more detailed, complex, sophisticated novels and poems requiring the reader to really *participate,* this was only raising the ante . . . escalating the *intensity* of the dosage. By participating . . . bring your cultural knowledge to bear no matter how obscure, you are actively helping the author to manipulate your mind. Thus, any popular novel or film that appeals to both kids and adults of both sexes and all backgrounds is like a new super-broad-spectrum antibiotic: everyone can take it and benefit from it . . . if they have coughs or sneezes, fevers or whatever, the drug will help . . . a novel or film of love and war, say, or a western, offers something for everybody . . . the all-purpose drug. If you "need" sadism, or sentiment, violence or tenderness, you simply extract that component, the way an ill body can extract the needed component from an all-purpose medicine like aspirin. In this way, the "intellectuals" become junkies.

And I literally saw all this . . . it all began to tumble out . . . as I stood in that bookstore being tempted to buy some books about the "true" experiences of interesting people! As a junkie, I finally in the later years could only mainline the pure stuff . . . if it was certified as *true* by the ads, dustjackets, book reviewers or critics, I would take it because that was, by definition to me, pure, and therefore it gave a greater high! In reality, of course, it's all just ink on paper! How could I know, really, what was or was not "true"; and worse yet, what an absolute insanity to think that the certification of true . . . i.e., reviewers word, or the small label "nonfiction," meant anything at all except what my mind wanted it to mean!

Critics and reviewers! It suddenly occurs to me (another item in the torrent of truth now) that such people are no more than sociocultural narcotics pushers.

Back to the bookstore again: I stood there, with these glimmerings flowing through me, and my skin beginning to prickle all over as I sensed what they meant. All around, wherever I looked, I was surrounded with the junk . . . the narcotics of the mind . . . sex, violence, heroisms, sadism, love, war, intellect, analysis, science, art . . . what, in fact, was not here represented? Every damned thing our whole Western culture has laboriously built up over centuries of mind manipulation!

Entertainment . . . diversion . . . symbols . . . facts (so called) of how to do everything. Emotions . . . history-philosophy-psychology-politics-*science*-adventure . . . all of it. What it does is put into one's mind the thoughts of others, which then prevent one from having one's own! It orients one to the experience and ideas derived from how others . . . the writers . . . have lived in their worlds, and it tends to prevent seeing of one's own way of being in the world. The art becomes the reality! No wonder it is so hard to achieve anything like what the masters call "suchness" . . . seeing the wonder of things as they are. Who can see and enjoy the fantastic multicolored bubbles in the dishwater when they are only waiting to get this dirty job done (how do you know it's dirty? because nobody ever wrote a novel about it except to call it dirty, right?) so they can get back to the TV, or the novel, or the great conversation or whatever it is they would *prefer* to do.

So I stood there *zonked;* surrounded by thousands of pushers, each silently beckoning me to get off on his or her path. Buy *this* and one could trip off on the World War II espionage path; buy *that* and learn the hidden secrets of Tibetan monasteries. It's all entertainments . . . dreams. No wonder the masters speak of enlightenment as "awakening"! No wonder the questions raised in zen training are always on the order of "What is your true nature?" "Find your true nature!" etc.

Who can find or know anything about themselves and the world they create for themselves moment by moment, when, like me, they have been avoiding themselves by diverting themselves, by *escaping* (through books, art, . . . even eating or sex) for the better part of their adult lives! And even as children! Hah! It's the first thing we learn, isn't it! To play with symbols! Insights tumble out again . . . only now it's about all those *theories* of developmental psychology. What they amount to is a kind of road map or triptych describing the mind diddlings and programmings, which, if carried out to sufficient extremes, allow one to be recognized as a grown-up . . . you can't be an adult until your ability to diddle your mind at a high level of symbolic complexity has been certified by a high school diploma. (Oh Ivan Illich . . . it's much worse than you said in "Deschooling"!)

Yes, we have to be able to manufacture reality according to the prevailing criteria of society before society will greet us with money, power, and all the goodies it has put in our minds that we want . . . *Playboy* bunnies, sports cars and the big ones . . . power, status . . . the ability to dominate people!

It goes on and on! I feel like I could sit at the typewriter for a year . . . for ten years . . . just recording the implications that keep falling out. Everything we thought *we* were doing was garbage!

Wow. We fall in love. What do we fall in love with? Real people? Oh no! It's the images and symbols! All of the women (how many? say about four, maybe five, that I have "loved" either in fact or in mind); all of them have been images of a certain kind of heroine. True. What heroine? Well, the "good sport." Forty years ago played in one film after another by Jean Arthur; and the tough world-weary, but underneath-it-all so loving woman played again forty years ago by . . . yessiree, old Marlene!

Of course, there are several kinds of imaginary heroines out there in addition to the good sport kinds. What do men of my stripe and generation really fall in love with? Well, anything that comes along that can talk and act tough; that gets turned on by big motorcycles, airplanes, and maybe a little war . . . enough at least so they can admire a man like me who actually volunteered himself into the infantry . . . and who, naturally, have great bodies, and really can dig the raunchiest kind of sex, while at the same time (and this is really crucial) knowing the right stuff: like eating chopped liver, and onions, and sardines; really good Jewish jokes, the right novelists like Papa Hemingway and old slick hair Fitzgerald (another dream maker whose stories never set me loose but whose life and essays really did it).

In short, one loves, or falls in love, with creatures who in certain critical ways share the same program, from their perspective on the anatomy chart of nature, of course, and who, above all, can provide on demand . . . orgasms. And *that,* my friends, is the bottom line on love and sex.

And everything else too. Having children, one wants to make them into everything one would have liked to be, right? All the things one learned to think of as ideal from those pushers and junk makers! Intellectuals. Artists. Men or women of action. Real shakers and movers.

Well . . . let us say simply that at long last one has discovered something important. Having in these past couple of hours walked about talking to myself aloud, hitting walls, drinking scotch, smoking too many cigarettes . . . because such an insight is hard to bear . . . I am now gonna stop it. On the edge of drunkenness.

I know one thing at least. Running and meditating. Two different things on the surface, but they are really just one: the way to get OUT of the mind put there by the pushers.

Aug. 21
COMING DOWN.   After a few days of no formal sitting at all, this morning a fifteen-minute period felt as near to perfect as I have ever thought possible . . . no small thing. The position was good, to begin with; a new sitting posture as earlier suggested by the instruction of a sore back, worked just splendidly. But more important than the posture is that finally, after such a long time, one has really learned something about how to do the meditation!

Thus, it is clear now that the beginning is critical: to quiet the mind by counting breathing is essential. But then, in addition to just observing the flights of thought, or wiping them out by striving to impose the state of empty-mindedness, it has emerged that one might also focus mind upon whatever disturbance is present . . . whatever infections, contaminations, or splatterings of mental junk obscure the clear mirror surface of mind. By focusing upon this, simply immersing in it, feeling the experience of the thing, one gains a clarity! The disturbing thing . . . whatever it might be . . . seemingly gets put in its place. After centering concentration on the experience, it gradually dissolves as one becomes calmly able to grasp the event in question . . . how it happened, where it came from, where it might be going, and most of all, the processes whereby it was allowed to happen, or one became vulnerable to it happening.

By meditating in this way, I have finally and very easily seemed to "get it." What? The truth that nothing can cloud or spot the clear mirror of mind unless we allow it to do so. That is, allow the thing to happen by taking part in the situation, by giving the situation its force through a mistaken, egotistical projection of our own mind energy (mind essence, the masters might say) into the scene. By opening ourselves in order to insert our own force into a situation, we become like someone attacking an aikido master, that is, we are providing the force which will be turned against us. Better yet, look at it this way: a person who walks with care and good concentration can hardly ever be tripped up by anything, whereas one who rushes forward ignoring the meaning of each footstep and looking only forward to some dimly seen goal, can hardly avoid tripping on their own feet, let alone the feet of others.

So meditation has now begun to open out and to flower in a new way. There is the empty mind form; the form focused on specific disturbances; and the form in which observation of thought is the salient activity. At least three general forms, and of course they may all be run together in a single sitting. In the past, for me, they have done so and been a source of confusion and misunderstanding leading to hardship in the practice. But now there is enough new clarity so that even when confusion occurs the elements in the confusion are clear. One knows, in short, much, much better where one is at in the action of the sitting. It's such a magnificent feeling. Like having been wandering around confused in the dark, and then having found a lamp lighting up a whole lot of what is out there. Darkness still at the periphery of the lamp light, naturally, but to one who has been in total or near total darkness for such a long time, to have got not merely a match or candle, but a regular lamp . . . well, it's like wow.

Aug. 23

FEELING BETTER

This feels very good:
Eating blueberry yogurt and reading zen.
This feels even better:
Just eating the yogurt and eating the yogurt.

Sept. 12
TDY IN THE CITIES.   A long gap in the record. For the past two weeks I have had to travel; Cape Cod via Boston airport.

New York via Interstate 95 from the Cape. Washington, D.C., via Metroliner from Penn Station. Back to the Great Plains via Interstate 70 from Washington.

If placed under the microscope of clear awareness, the travels of these weeks might easily make a book . . . so much seeing and doing. Also some running, some snatches here and there of meditation. They both served well enough to prevent some of the worst of my previous activities on such occasions: self-indulgences arising from intellectual arrogance and professional competition, not to mention overdoing the eating, drinking, smoking, talking. But whatever little progress may be seen in the better praxis of this trip, it seems as nothing compared with the profound disgusts experienced. Disgusts at the environments, the people in them, the activities and practices observed.

Yet even this seems pale in comparison with the realization that such reflexive disgusts are in themselves clear indications of just how small a distance I have been able to advance. It is very obvious that one who had made truly significant progress would not feel or be open to the feelings of disgust; would not automatically tick off people as worthless trash, or be so oppressed by the sense of imperial decadence permeating Washington, and commercial corruption strangling New York.

The return to this small town of clean air and clear skies is as a return to some religious refuge. It would not be such a relief for one of true enlightenment. It is clear, therefore, that I still need the refuge, and will not venture away from it again unless pressed by very serious circumstances. The entire episode leaves behind it an apathetic sadness, a flat, awed wonder at the sheer waste and futility. How can one feel anything else after seeing so many people killing themselves in so many ingenious ways as they ride so fully committed to the wheel of karma?

10 BEING STUCK

THE BURN-OUT. For some time now, ever since returning from the trip noted earlier, it has been impossible to record anything. The meditation record has been virtually blank, both in terms of doing and thinking. What has happened is that everything has come to a standstill, at least so far as the original and evolving intent of this recording effort is concerned. There is nothing left to write on the subject because somehow or other, I have become empty on the subject.

To put it very simply, one now finds oneself in yet another different place from where one started. It is so different that the whole flow of experienced meaning that was to constitute this record is gone. It just went away somewhere; either I lost it, or it lost me. About a week ago, the realization emerged one nice morning that this thing was finished. I can't record where I am now because I don't know where it is, and I don't have words to describe it.

There *are* words, of course, but they are totally inadequate. One could steal the words of the old masters and suggest that with this new feeling nothing matters . . . that one exists without imperatives, or better, that all the imperatives, including whatever it was (some form of ego indulgence?) that inspired this effort to record the experience of meditation . . . well, it's gone away.

During the past couple of weeks this realization has become clearer and clearer. It's rather like a taste change: one remembers vividly loving a certain food, and then discovers that one doesn't any more. At first, it seems very surprising. And confusing. One tries it again and again, but the taste, the pleasure, is just not there. This is what has been happening, and it's been happening in all sorts of ways that are surprising, confusing, and even just now becoming a little frightening because of the implications.

Some examples; just for the record (a statement that now seems amusing and quaint, like something from a remote past). All sorts of things that used to seem, if not important, then at least worth doing, no longer seem that way. I go to see the occasional good film, highly recommended and very well reviewed, and I fall asleep. In fact, it seems that the better the film, the more I see it as a boring, artificial foolishness. The same with books. It didn't surprise me that I couldn't read novels with the same old pleasure any more. That has been true for a couple of years now. And the growing indifferences to *non*fiction, again, even the very best quality stuff, has also been no great surprise. But now the pattern has come to include material quite relevant to my work, and worse yet, even the good zen writings that I relied upon until a few weeks ago.

What's happened in this latter case is something like this: the good stuff I recognize immediately as good is apparent, obvious and manifest, and, therefore, rather dull. (How can this be explained? Before, when the writing of a master in effect pointed down to the ground and said "See the glow of the sun here" one was curious because one had thought the sun was up in the sky. Now, one knows . . . it doesn't matter . . . the sun might be anywhere or nowhere . . . and one is inwardly responding with a shrug, a smile of recognition. And a "Yes, that's the way it is, all right.")

Then there is professional work. It's not necessary to have zen, or dialectics, or any other metaphysical belief system in order to know that work should not be taken too seriously. Certainly any good craftsman of anything comes to know this when his skill is far enough advanced so that his work is no longer alien or artificial, but reflexive. A good craftsman can merge with his work the way a good motorcycle rider merges with his machine, and the result in both cases is the same: he transcends the thing and takes it very lightly, easily, like breathing. I used to consider such a realization or insight to be very profound; now I know it is quite trivial, an obvious fact of life. There has grown in the past few weeks a deeper conviction that work itself is nothing. The career, the reputation for good quality performance and fulfillment of commitments, etc., all the stuff that professional craftsmanship is made of, is all just another obviously transitory, artificial bubble of illusion. It's just another way of staying plugged into the Great American Dream Machine, another way of indulging the ego according to shared values that help to keep the machine wound up and running. It is, finally, just another, higher form of masturbation.

But I am stuck. Really at a standstill because I don't have what it takes to act on this knowledge. At the moment, certain commitments remain outstanding. There are certain deadlines to meet, projects to complete. Other people; honorable, decent and "good," as one has carefully rationed out these terms to the very few, are dependent upon me to fulfill my commitments. I also know this is all baloney; there are no such things, it doesn't matter, and in the end whether or not I do as expected makes no great odds one way or the other. (Like I could die tomorrow and the whole machine, dependents and all, might give a slight burp or stutter but would continue right on.) So, knowing all this with a profound, clear sense of its truth, is to know that all the pride of commitment, craftsmanship, of not letting the side down, is just so much crap-illusion. Yet I am stuck because I can't go ahead and contradict all of it.

The only way out seems to be to fulfill the current set of commitments, which include legal as well as moral contracts, and then not take on any more. But this is only more nonsense. I know that the wheel of activity will continue to turn, and that it will *always* be just as hard to get off, to say no, as it is right now. So here I am, stuck in the dilemma of knowing that it is time to say no, but not being able to do it. It's what we used to call a Mexican standoff.

Along the same line, in a more personal context there has come full realization that "caring" or "loving" is also just another ego illusion. Caring leads to trying. One tries to help in every way possible those one cares about, loves. And the result is never anything except a laying upon them of one's own ego trip. To be trying to show them better ways, instruct them in their mistakes, demonstrate to them that they can be better, help them advance, give them pleasure, and so on and so forth; it's all crap. What one is really doing is projecting the same kind of egotistical illusions upon others as do the exploitative, domineering bastards of the world who hate instead of love. One is dealing here with two sides of the same coin. All that loving instruction and careful caring is just another way of putting strings on people, another way of projecting into them and onto them one's own personal and very fallible experience of the world. And implicitly, it is also a way of demanding the same thing in return, even though one might think otherwise.

The truth is simple: you can't do anything really important for anyone else. The best thing is to stop trying. The only way to stop trying is to stop caring. But, one can't quite stop caring, so one is stuck. Some of the masters indicate, in obscure ways, that it may be possible to achieve some sort of dialectical state of caring-while-not caring. Maybe. Maybe it's like riding a cycle at very high speeds. One cares about getting killed, yet one doesn't care, because if one did, one wouldn't ride at high speeds. But this is no real help at all. It's just a vague little glimmer.

The list of things that are stuck now could go on and on. In addition to not caring, there is also not winning. It came to me playing tennis the other day. For more than twenty-five years of my life the game has meant winning. One is supposed to try to win. And with a few minor exceptions for children, cripples or whatnot, I always have tried. Even though it doesn't matter . . . nobody is keeping score, nobody cares, least of all me. So why not, if one can't give up trying, do the opposite? If trying is one of the bonds fixing one to the wheel of repetitive, meaningless activity, then why not try "not-trying"? So far, I've only tested this once by letting go and losing when I might have won, and it feels very funny. Will have to see how it goes.

More important, though, a whole great bunch of ordinary practices of life are beginning to seem like the tennis situation. Every day is filled with all sorts of unexamined, taken-for-granted-as-positive tryings. And now it is clear that my path has led to a place where the only important thing to try is not trying.

What it is, then, is that the whole structure, the whole internal skeletal structure of how one has lived is crumbling to pieces. It's like standing back and watching an old building being demolished. Pieces keep falling off; beams and girders are steadily being blown away. So many illusions: science is an elaborate magic act. As one has got to be a master at it one has discovered all the tricks. And language is the patter, the diversion that enables the hand to move quicker than the eye. One's life is a portrait painting full of imperatives that are only arbitrary, false strokes. There are no imperatives, and the portrait is phony, just a matter of social aesthetics . . . the comforts and self-indulgences. I'm stuck in it.

So this record ends here. This is where the meditation has brought me. There is a final thing to say about it, however: clear vision. This means that among other things, stuck though one is, there is a clear penetrating vision of other people; a seeing right through their outer practices, words, behaviors, into their skeletal structure of illusion. People seem utterly transparent. Their actions seem more and more simply and obviously to result from the cultural ego strings that are attached to them . . . their values! What an extraordinary joke! There is no particular contempt here, only a clear comprehension of the way people are doing their lives, or letting their lives be done to them by the various cultural wire pullers (ideas and ideals) they hold to be true.

So the question is, where do we go from here, boys? Don't know. I'm stuck and all I can do is wait until I get unstuck, one way or another. Maybe I'll get used to all the things that have me stuck. Already, in very small ways, some changes seem to be settling in, like trying to lose at tennis. *How to Play Losing Tennis*. I could maybe write a book under that title. But I know with real certainty that this is going to be a very strange period. Getting unstuck, if I ever do, is going to take an as-yet unknowable effort . . . which may be no effort at all. It will take a long time too. These past few weeks have made that much very obvious. I don't think I can get really unstuck without making profound changes in personal life as well as work. And I can't make such changes without hurting people a lot, even though I know their pain will only be fundamentally the pain of punctured illusions . . . of seeing that what they have taken for granted as fixed and immutable is only arbitrary . . . an act of their will as it has been an act of mine. From here on, it's a matter of learning to live with nothing . . . in limbo. Some of the masters, I think, have called this sort of thing the Great Death.

SEPT. 27
POSTSCRIPT FROM LIMBO.   Everything written in

the prior entry is correct, but it is also only partial in its correctness. To explain all of it as I feel and know all of it would require yet another volume, and a disgusting one at that, because it would be composed of tedious word-quibbles: definitions, implications, explications, and all that *dreck* of intellectualism. What should be recorded, instead, are the events of one's life in limbo.

Yesterday, instead of the usual Sunday morning tennis, I ran a very slow, very satisfying, and very long way, approximately ten miles. One thing left is my absurd Mt. Everest run; the koan that emerged several weeks ago. It's nice to have. One may think of it, know it's there waiting, and go on preparing. The fall trial should be fairly soon now because yesterday's run felt strong, like maybe I could make it through.

This morning, because of some errands, it was convenient to run the four cylinder Honda. Haven't been out on it much for a week. It turned into a superb ride. Instead of going on to work, I took it out for another hour at high speeds, and when, finally, it was time to come in, "Bingo!" A very bad skid at an intersection. Just enough leeway to pull out of it before hitting a concrete divider strip, but it was only a matter of two feet either way, as between pulling out and going down. This kind of thing hasn't happened to me in quite a long time, and it suggests that things in general may be getting down to basics. The dangers of being stuck are perhaps becoming much more manifest and concrete than I had thought possible. What a curious turn of events!

11 BIRD DROPPINGS

DEC. 23

THE PAIN GURU.   Pain and death are the two certainties of life, absolute certainties compared to which every other event in life is only a possibility or probability. Zen knows this as the Buddha knew it, and as all great prophets, mystics, and religious creators have known it. But whereas all religions teach this to people and then offer them a set of illusions—heaven, hell, gods, reincarnations, magics of all varieties—Zen only teaches it very indirectly in a way that breaks down a person's thirst for illusions. And so, if a person finally comes to a true feeling and reflexive understanding of life (viz: death and pain) through zen practice, they want no new illusions and they are done with illusions forever. This has such profound effects upon their life praxis, their thinking, and their very being-in-the-world, that other people often think they are either mad, or in possession of some extraordinary mystical secret.

The severity, harsh discipline, and mental (koan work) and physical (zazen posture, menial chores) suffering required of all those who practice zen, are neither mysterious nor arbitrary. Instead, they are the time-honored ways that have been discovered as the best instruction permitting people to realize for themselves the true character of life. The beauty of such training is that it not only reveals the great truth, but also shows how one may cope with knowing this truth; how to conduct oneself.

Thus, what seems bizarre becomes superbly simple. If a Zennist were to say to me, "What is your understanding?" or, more indirectly in accord with a traditional alternative statement of the same question: "What did Dharma bring from the West?" or "Why did Dharma come from the West?" etc., then I might in the past have replied with many words and thereby shown very little grasp of the way of zen because of being still caught up in the abstractions, illusions, and falsifications of reality that language imposes.

More recently, as my grasp became stronger, I might have replied simply by saying "running and sitting," for these have been my two practices while studying the writings of the masters. Moreover, having eventually realized that both practices were one thing, namely different entryways or gates to the same great truth of pain, death, and the mode of conduct or praxis that comes along with this knowledge, I would be confident in my statement. The questioner, in turn, would perceive this, and recognize the authenticity of my answer partly because running and sitting are both "severe" activities, but even more importantly, because the authenticity would be confirmed by my being. My appearance would show immediately that I run. My whole style of conduct— movements, tone of voice, manner of breathing, complexion— would reveal me as a runner. And the same sort of cues would affirm my practice of sitting; one who has put in substantial practice of sitting with absolute stillness in zazen meditation does not fidget about, twist or squirm, and there are other signs as well.

If the questioner were a true master and concerned to move me toward a still deeper grasp of zen by discovering my present boundary or frontier of enlightenment, the answer "running and sitting" might provoke a further remark indicating, in the traditionally indirect fashion, that my sitting practice was not nearly as advanced as my running. My conduct and appearance would have made this apparent to the master. A truly great master might even then reach out and twist my nose very harshly, or deliver a powerful slap to my face, and as I blinked dazedly, the master might say: "Show me your running and sitting!" or, "The rock over there neither runs nor sits." At this point, recognizing the greater truth expressed by the master, as well as the intent of the action taken to convey it, I might close our dialogue by bowing deeply. On the other hand, if I sensed that the master was demonstrating his own limit of enlightenment (as could be the case if I had been struck in a way that seemed less than fully confident!), or if I wanted to show that I could not only recognize his action but also challenge it by asserting a further advanced stage of knowledge, I might respond to the blow with a full-hearted smile and invitation to "Have a cup of tea." Or better, if the master were an American, I could say, "There is a place around the corner that has wonderful pizza." This latter remark would indicate an invitation to eat together in affirmation, so to speak, of our mutual recognition of each other.

But returning to the thematic question, I now believe that a more elegant, simple, and meaningful reply to it would be for me to reach out and slowly twist the questioner's nose, or pinch his arm. This would be a much better way of showing my knowledge of the great truth because it would not depend upon words, such as "running and sitting," but would demonstrate the truth of pain very directly. Moreover, it would bypass the instruments or vehicles of my understanding (the running and sitting) and instead show precisely what these activities have revealed to me. And if the questioner were a great master, my action would be affirmed by some counteraction such as either a softer or harder pinch, or an invitation to tea.

This is the way zen proceeds, and it is virtually impossible for anyone to participate in it unless they are ready to deal directly with fundamental reality.

ZEN TRUTH

I lived more than forty years in this world
without any true awareness.

Life has only two certainties: pain and death.
Unknowing, I was mostly unhappy, disturbed,
and a source of unhappiness and disturbance to others.
Now that I am aware of the truth
I am mostly happy, undisturbed, and
not a source of unhappiness and disturbance to others.

DEC. 27
MINDFULNESS OF MIND.

Sudden pain snaps the mind away from its everlasting verbal and pictorial constructions of meaning. The falsification of immediate reality is apparently the chief work of mind.

In formal zen practice, some schools make important use of the fact that sudden, surprising pain will break the mind flow, the so-called stream of consciousness Hence the masters developed a tradition whereby one monk passes among the others during their meditation period, and at any sign of slackness, strikes them forcefully with a length of bamboo. Those receiving the blow bow in formal acknowledgment that it was given as an aid to their practice, and that it is a useful means of yanking the mind out of its tendency toward verbal-visual imaginings.

Mindfulness of mind, mental discipline and control is terribly difficult to achieve.

FEB. 5
AIKIDO OF THE MIND.

It's been a long time coming, and of course, as usual it came only after one had given up and forgotten already that one had given up, but today "It" dropped another bolt of knowledge into me: Bang! Like that.

In the meditation that I hang onto despite all failings of regular discipline, gaps, falls backward, etc., there has lately been just dimly noticed a change in the flow and dynamics of thought while sitting. In the past, it was needful to use breathing, and counting of breathing, as an instrument—a blunt club of an instrument often enough—for beating down the thoughts of fame and gain or aggression, hostility, and self-righteous, self-justifying monologues.

Lately, there has been less of that, because those low-level thought scenarios have been receding a little into the less salient contours of mind. Those old, familiar ego-thoughts are less imperative, less domineering, and *mindfulness* is accordingly easier to maintain.

Today, ego-thoughts of hostility were prominent when first entering the meditation. Without special concern, however, I brought out the breath-counting and used it to get quiet (like a grade-school teacher calling unruly kids to order!). Well and good. But then other, less intrusive thoughts came in: of an old Woody Guthrie song and of some friends. Easy background sorts of thoughts. And these began to mix in together with the now-beaten-down thoughts of hostility, forming a backdrop to the meditation like a Mozart quartet. A better image is that the mixed thoughts seemed like a bunch of different fish all swimming around together in a glass tank. In any case, it became possible then to detach and observe everything going on in the fish-tank of mind.

Quite astonishing! One can recognize the experience because the masters have written about it. But this was not all. What then followed in an even more astonishing way was that I could play or "call" the fish! That is, out of the myriad of thoughts various individuals could be called forward, and they could even be called up in pairs and triplets to confront one another.

Now that's potent! One can call up, or arrange entities of thought and pit them against one another. And thus one can dominate without effort. Arrayed against each other, the single thoughts lose their power of domination! Then it came in another flash: this is the divide and conquer strategy; this is how you split the atom!

So now I know something totally new: the way to break through the oppressive walls of ego. It is rather like that early perceptual experience of seeing separately out of each eye. But now it can be done with thoughts! To know this is to know how to get out—get free, whenever one wants to. Like a prisoner who has found a secret tunnel allowing escape at will. Yes indeed. The walls of ego come tumbling down.

This is aikido of the mind, whereby forceful but intrusive thoughts can be diverted away from self, and the greater their force, the easier it is to divert them into one another, and thus be free of them.

FEB. 25
DEEP DISGUSTS. As the practice of mindfulness increases, intensifies, and extends out in different directions, accumulated layers of *disgusts* are starting to loosen up and come to the surface of awareness.

For the past few weeks, practice has come to include food and cigarettes. It might be described as follows. Whatever new energy of mind is now available, and there seems to be quite a bit, it is sufficient to support a serious focus of attention on eating and smoking habits. Using this energy, it is possible for the first time to work on the tyranny of the appetites. And so I have managed recently to eliminate meats and sugar from my diet. The details are unimportant, except to say that this is a real change that has brought a clear increase in energy. The new feeling of well-being, in turn, has brought with it the conviction that I might go further and attack cigarette smoking.

Having smoked a pack a day for about twenty-five years; having also failed to reduce it, let alone stop it, I have been living with it as a kind of untouchable, in the sense that come what may (cancer or whatever) there was nothing to be done. In theory, of course, it has been clear that to tackle this addiction would require immense energy. That is, one could always stop by working up an oppressive, fear-inspired set of desperate emotions, but what I wanted was something else: to stop or seriously reduce the smoking in a harmonious fashion. It has not been possible, however, until just recently . . . the past few days. Now it is working. I am stopping while keeping cigarettes all around me, and in the few days of this effort consumption has been cut to half what it was. Moreover, this change is permanent. It feels completely authentic and, for want of a better word, harmonious.

So much for the background. The main event has been the welling up into consciousness of deep-seated disgusts . . . one has the sense of seeing more clearly inside oneself and into the activities of the immediate environment . . . and the result is a greatly heightened awareness of disgusting mental and emotional worthlessness. It seems also that by reducing the food and the smoking indulgences one sees the *reasons* for these self-indulgences revealed in all their bitter clarity. The rich foods and smoking are the means one has used to adapt to the disgusts in oneself and others! It seems so obvious: one reaches for cigarettes to cope with tension, to help swamp some feeling of disharmony. And foods, whether the tempting sweets or the rich beefsteaks or wonderfully seasoned sauce-covered anythings, are an even more directly obvious way of drugging the senses. Especially when taking large amounts.

By not using these means of getting along with the disgusts, one sees them and feels them much more keenly, including the layers that are deeply down inside oneself. It's a revelation, at first very surprising but then more and more obviously to be expected, to discover how much layered *dreck* is down there in the well of my being. It had seemed earlier on that the bottom of the well was pretty much cleaned up: heaven knows, one had been hauling out buckets of junk quite regularly for a couple of years! And now, all of a sudden there is a whole new pile of it to be moved. Wow! It is damn-near awe-inspiring. Like getting to the bottom of a lake or swimming pool only to find that the bottom is false, and that there is a whole new, and for-all-you-can-tell *infinite* depth of water to be explored. Ah well, the work is never done, and besides, who wants to get to the final bottom? Yet it's a big surprise to find out that one has been living on top of this bottomless pit of garbage; garbage so impacted and so deep that it isn't until the horrible-smelling surface layers have been removed a bit that one knows what's really under there. One took it for solid rock all these years, and now, close-up inspection reveals only smelly quicksand!

Mar. 2
CHARLIE CHAPLIN.   The final emotion . . . is not, after all, just disgust. Beyond it is calm, detached wonder and giggly amusement following from precise *scrutiny* of the disgust. That actor out there called SELF! What an endlessly inventive verbal monkey . . . dancing on and on, always in the dark, and always trying to outperform the other monkeys on the playground apparatus we call culture. No wonder Charlie Chaplin could become an archetype.

MAR. 7
A BALANCE SHEET.   Running and sitting do these things for you:

They teach and instruct in the workings of pain; they reduce the mind-trips of fame and gain. Then the appetites begin to be approachable . . . sex and food. One may get to be able to work with them too, the way one works with one's body in yoga efforts. Last of all, even cigarettes are finally being managed. The cigarette tyrant is not gone, but is quite tamed down from its former power.

At first I thought it meant "revolution." Instead of living in thrall to pain-fears, appetite-desires, and the addiction, one could instead master *them*. Turn the tables! Revolutionize and make a ruthless extermination of those exploitative kulaks of mind and body!

What nonsense! The Buddha truth is "not two," right enough, but it's also "not one, either."

So one doesn't master and ruthlessly exterminate anything . . . not even the classical "bad habits" of mind and body. No, really what one can do is learn to live in harmony and pleasure with them! Food and sex and pain and perhaps even smoking too, with all their sources in the emotional greeds, all of them are nothing when one is neither dominated by them *nor driven by ego to eradicate all of them!* Instead, we need to play with them according to our own rules emerging from our own practices. This is how we can begin to enjoy our own harmonies and contradictions.

Take a final metaphor here: my greeds, fears of pain, hungers of body and demands for satiation, pleasure, all of them and all of their manifestations, are now beginning to look a lot like a team of baseball players. I can't get all the players to do everything I want whenever I want, but like a fair manager I can call some plays, and at least decide when the team should go out on the field and who should be where in the batting order! (Not bad, coach . . . we play for the pennant in the Buddha-League this year!)

MAR. 9
THE HUMAN SUBMARINE.   I used to think of entering meditation as submerging. Now I think of it as rising to the surface.

Mar. 14

It has developed lately that work on the body ought to proceed much further. What has been learned, somehow, mainly by seeing a living example of someone getting into the full lotus position, is that by working harder to assimilate more pain, I can get my body much closer to the full lotus than ever before. The position now being reached for the first time is still far from the lotus, yet at the same time it is much closer than would have seemed remotely possible a few months ago. One can work with the pain of it.

Why is the lotus such a big deal? I think it must be this: if one can master it, then one is mastering the body in such a way that severe pain is being mastered. And when this can be achieved, then liberation from much of body tyranny can be achieved. It is very simple, and it is shocking to think that something so obvious was never understood before.

(Today, having got further toward the lotus than ever, and held on to the position reasonably well for a time, I uttered a deep, spontaneous "Om!" It felt very good.)

Mar. 15

In Western religious-philosophical tradition, it is held that the individual may struggle to give up vices, to achieve purity or grace. In the Buddhist tradition, it is held that if the individual cultivates "correct practices," the vices will give up of their own accord.

Since going about without carrying cigarettes, I am less able to tolerate or to bear situations of stupidity and/or frustration, and so I leave them sooner than before. That is, before I used to light a cigarette out of boredom or frustration, whereas now, that desire to light a cigarette and the inability to do so serves as a perfectly clear instruction that it is time to get out . . . an unforeseen benefit!

Mar. 24

LOVERS OF NATURE

Nature has many lovers
When she is not too dry or too wet,

Too hot or too cold,
And when she is prepared to satisfy
Their fantasies.

APR. 2

All the travels, the wanderings and pilgrimages so prominent in
mystical literature and storytelling, are really no more than
metaphors for the changing events of mind. Our travels, searches
and discoveries are all in the mind. How can one know this, speak
with certainty about it? Because the past few weeks of following
new and more intensive and more or less "secret" practices (sharp
reduction in cigarettes, meat, sugar; increase of yoga, meditation,
and running) has begun to noticeably carry me into another
country . . . yet another country by damn—of the mind.

It feels wonderful: increased energy, sharper focus, and a
greatly expanded feeling of freedom. Yet not one single thing aside
from my personal practice has changed. And the elements of the
practice are hardly known to anyone except me! Odd, and even a
little amusing: one feels to be somewhat like a secret agent living in
the body of the person one used to be. Well-briefed, the agent
knows the whole life history and all the cover stories. He can even
manifest typical behavior patterns like an honors graduate from
the Actor's Studio!

Interesting too that at the moment, the yoga work recently
taken up and aimed at accomplishing a full lotus and a full
headstand is quite stymied! Despite working at them day after day
there is no substantial progress. Sometimes even a feeling of loss of
progress. But here now is a clear characteristic of the new country·
of the mind: I find it all very amusing and not upsetting or
frustrating at all. In fact, it seems good to have something to work
at that one cannot do and perhaps never will! Falling out of the
attempted headstand position, for example, is really funny; and
making even a momentary millimeter of progress in it, or in the
lotus, is immensely satisfying. Thus all is perfectly good, perfectly
in order. The "I" that's left in me just doesn't care much one way or
the other because it doesn't matter. Why do it then, if it doesn't
matter? I don't know. I just think it's good to do—helpful—
productive of good feeling and energy—and that is all, since the

good feelings from *trying* the positions don't have anything to do with *accomplishing* the positions.

APR. 5
LIVING HIGH.   Everyday life is becoming more and more like an exceptionally deep, rich, natural high. A week has gone by with *no* meat, no sugar to speak of, little smoking, reduced eating, more running and more sitting. Result? A superb four-to-five-mile run this morning (40 degrees; wet streets after a rainstorm) that felt like nothing ever before. Sheer power inside; like there was a super-charged battery just glowing in the interior and letting me pull out as much energy as I wanted without showing any significant depletion. And after the run, for the past forty-five minutes of cooling out and then sitting, dead silent, there still remains this feeling of having a great ball of electrical energy inside. It is accompanied by joy; a pure sense of happiness in being just as one is . . . No "reason" or logic here. One hears music in the mind . . . feels perfect rhythms and exquisite balance moving about . . . and perfect clarity of mind. The description of mind that springs forward spontaneously from the writings of the masters is: "cleansed perception," and, just for the record, let it be noted here that it is an utterly beautiful sensation. One feels too that if death were to come suddenly out of nowhere it could be greeted with a genuine smile. Nothing at all: *bon appétit,* take whatever you want, jive-ass!

12 DOINGS OF THE MIND

RECREATION. The only real difference between washing up a sink full of dirty dishes and skiing down Riva's Ridge at Vail in a foot of new light powder, radiant in morning sunlight, is this: doings of the mind!

JUSTICE. There is no justice, there are only approximations to equity, which is a quantitative idea, whereas justice means that people get what they deserve, a very *qualitative* idea, and hence impossible of achievement except in the mind.

A HAIKU FOR CHRISTMAS

Some people have brown mouths from speaking too much, and others from swallowing too much.

Despite Jesus (and Buddha and Moses and Marx and Freud),
they do not know where the brown comes from.

This is why we have psychiatrists and lawyers.

**ON CORRESPONDING WITH A BRILLIANT
IVY LEAGUE SCHOLAR.** He uses his intellect freely
and with great style, the way Errol Flynn used women and whiskey.
Is it possible to become addicted to one's own performance of
conceptual thinking the way others become addicted to booze,
golf, grass, or sex?

MORALITY. Modern psychiatry has destroyed the Western
idea of morality by revealing that if a person is willing to sacrifice
himself for some higher value . . . moral or otherwise . . . they are
also usually willing to sacrifice others.

CLINGING

Clinging to the idea of life makes death hard, and life hard.
Clinging to the idea of death makes life easy, and death easy.

FUNGUS. The doings of mind are so ubiquitous that we
forget we inhabit this body contraption with all its strange,
complex apparatus, and all its bizarre mechanical, electrical, and
chemical activities. At one end it is subject to athletes foot; at the
other to dandruff. Indeed, mysterious fungus attaches to us the
way moss grows on rocks and tiny sea life on whales.

MEDITATION. The most important thing to know about
meditation is that the point is to observe the contents and flow of
mind and not worry or inquire who or what is doing the observing.
Just do it.

AMERICAN ZEN: COULDS AND SHOULDS.

American Zen could appreciate the form and knowledge of old Japanese temples and monasteries, but should know that to imitate them is only to imitate them.

American Zen could understand the aesthetics of old Japanese priestly robes and garments, but should know that to wear them is only play-acting.

American Zen could shave its head and sit in the lotus and grow its own vegetables like the old Japanese monks, but should know that it has yet to find its own practices.

American Zen could study the form and substance of the Rinza and Soto Ways, but should know this is not an end, only a beginning.